Betrayed

by

Carl Taylor

Cornelsen

Betrayed

erarbeitet von
Carl Taylor M.A., Maidencombe, Devon

Umschlag
Hewett Street Studios, London: Liz Roberts

Cornelsen online
http://www.cornelsen.de

1. Auflage €
Druck 14 13 12 11 Jahr 05 04 03 02

Alle Drucke dieser Auflage sind inhaltlich unverändert und können im Unterricht nebeneinander verwendet werden.

Druck: Saladruck, Berlin

ISBN 3-464-05330-X

Bestellnummer 53300

Gedruckt auf säurefreiem Papier,
umweltschonend hergestellt aus chlorfrei gebleichten Faserstoffen.

Chapter One

A large, silver-grey car rolled quietly into the grounds of Hartlands School and stopped outside the main office. It was the middle of the afternoon and not many people could be seen. Some pupils who were late for their afternoon lessons looked curiously at the large car to see if it was a visitor they knew or possibly a new pupil before they ran to their classrooms. A cleaner came out of the main building, but she ignored the car. Such vehicles were nothing new at Hartlands. The woman who got out of the car was brown from the sun, healthy and well-dressed. She looked over the school grounds. She had seen them before when she had visited the school to talk to the headmaster. She had liked Hartlands then and she liked it now: the old buildings, the lovely gardens with their many different flowers, the trees and the lawns where pupils could sit and talk. It was a lovely corner of England, very beautiful and very peaceful. Thomas should like it here, she thought, and walked towards the main office. She said nothing to the young boy who was sitting on the back seat, looking sadly out of the car window.

For Thomas time seemed to stand still. Nothing moved. The school became a picture, something he could look at carefully from the car window because he was not yet part of it; he didn't know what was behind the walls or who was in the different rooms. He sat quietly and waited, and time passed. How much he didn't know, but then suddenly a bell rang and life awoke around him. Boys and girls of all ages came out of the buildings and went in all directions. Pupils shouted, ran after each other, kicked footballs, stood or sat in groups. Some looked into the car and he felt like a monkey in the zoo. Frightened, he sat further down in the seat and waited nervously for his mother. But before she came, another bell rang and he watched with interest as the pupils walked away in different groups to different buildings, until the grounds were as quiet again as they had been some minutes before.

The car door opened and his mother said, "Thomas, you can get out now."

He climbed out of the car. He felt strange. He was in a place he didn't know. This could never be his home. "This is Mr Clay. He's a teacher here. He will show us round the school and then we will go to your room. Mr Clay will also look after you if you have any problems."

Thomas looked at the teacher. He was a young man. He seemed to be nice and friendly.

"Hallo, Thomas," said Mr Clay.

"Hallo, sir," said Thomas quietly. And he followed his mother and his new teacher on a tour of the school. As they walked along the paths, it seemed to Thomas that she was the new pupil and not he.

* * *

When they arrived back at the car, his mother opened the doors and they took out his things. Everything he owned was carefully packed in these boxes and bags, his favourite clothes, his books, records and cassettes, posters to put on the walls, photo albums, the contents of his short life.

They walked towards a large building while Mr Clay talked to his mother.

"We have put everybody in small groups of about eight or nine pupils. We call these groups 'families'. One teacher looks after each group and helps the pupils with their school work, their homework or with their personal problems. We also make sure that pupils wash regularly and change their socks."

He smiled at Thomas. But Thomas looked away, embarrassed. It was obviously important to wear clean socks at Hartlands.

"And Thomas will be in your family?"

"That's right. His room will be in Warren House. I have a flat on the same floor, so he can come to me at all times."

"I hope you heard that Thomas," his mother said.

"Yes," he replied and they walked through two huge wooden doors into a very old building. After the afternoon sun he found it dark inside.

"We have about 60 boys in Warren House," said Mr Clay. "They are on two floors. Downstairs is the Lower Dormitory. That is for the older boys. The younger boys in Thomas's age group are upstairs in the Upper Dormitory."

They started to climb the wide wooden stairs. Everything in the school was old. It even smelt old. Upstairs, they came to a very long dark corridor. It frightened Thomas to see it. He wondered if prisoners felt like this when they were led to their cells. The only light came from a small window at the far end. On both sides of the corridor were the doors to the pupils' rooms. Between the doors were huge wooden wardrobes at least eight feet tall. They leaned dangerously against the walls as if they were too tired to stand and might fall down any minute. Generations of pupils had kicked them and damaged them, written their names on their wooden sides with their knives, and still they stood and would still be there, as solid as ever, when the next generations came.

Mr Clay switched the electric lights on and the corridor became a little brighter. "This isn't the most attractive place in the school," he said. "We hope to paint and decorate the whole building later this year. The pupils can, of course, decorate or paint their rooms as they wish." They stopped outside a door. Thomas noticed the name Ralph Jenkins on a white card.

"Two or three pupils share a room. Each room has a lock and each pupil gets a key to his room. In this way the rooms are the private area of the pupil. This is one of the smaller rooms so Thomas will only share it with one other boy."

Mr Clay knocked on the door before he opened it. Inside, Thomas saw a bright, comfortable room. Ralph was sitting at his table near the window, where he was doing his homework. Music was coming softly from a small radio on a shelf. Posters were on the walls. But there was another corner that was empty. An empty bed, an empty table, empty bookshelves. This was his area.

"Ralph, this is Thomas Walker. He'll be your new roommate."

Ralph stood up, smiled and said hallo. Thomas's mother smiled back and placed her son's bags on the empty bed. She looked around the room as if it was a test and she had to give it points. She decided quickly. "I'm sure you'll feel at home, Thomas."

"I'm sure he will," said Mr Clay.

Thomas stood where he was and said nothing. He felt shy and nervous. The other boy, Ralph, sat down again and continued with his homework. He had his area. He had taken about two-thirds of the room. The new boy could do what he wanted with the other third.

"Well," said Thomas's mother. "I suppose the best thing is if you start to unpack." She turned to Mr Clay. "I suppose it will soon be time for evening meal."

"At half past six," said Mr Clay. "Ralph will show Thomas where he must go."

"Yes, sir," said Ralph

"Fine," said his mother.

"Well," said Mr Clay, "while Thomas is unpacking, may I show you more of the school? Or perhaps you would like to stay for evening meal?"

"No, thank you. Really. I must leave soon. I'll quickly bring the rest of his things from the car."

They walked out and left Thomas with his bags and boxes and a small empty area that from now on was his home.

"Why are you here?" asked Ralph, a little friendlier now that the teacher and the mother had gone.

"My parents live abroad," said Thomas.

"Can't you live with them?"

Thomas shook his head.

"How old are you?"

"I'll be 15 this year."

"Same as me. Mr Clay said you'll be in the same class that I'm in."

But then the door flew open and a pupil walked in. He was tall with blond hair and older than the other two boys.

"Hey, Jenkins. I need a French dictionary."

"I'm using mine," said Ralph. "Ask somebody else."

But the pupil walked up to Ralph's desk. "I'm asking you."

He took the dictionary and started to leave the room.

"Who's this?"

"A new pupil," said Ralph.

The older boy looked at him and walked out. He left the door open.

* * *

Outside in the corridor a loud voice shouted. "Bradley. What are you doing here?"

"Just borrowed a dictionary," came the answer.

The two boys heard loud steps in the corridor outside and a teacher suddenly stood in the open doorway. He was larger than Mr Clay, much older and seemed to be very strict.

"What did Bradley want?"

"He just wanted a dictionary," said Ralph.

"Why did he come here?"

"I don't know, sir."

The teacher walked into the room and looked carefully round. Then he turned to Thomas.

"Are you the new boy?"

Thomas nodded.
"You'd better unpack quickly. It'll soon be time for evening meal."
"Yes, sir," said Thomas.
The teacher left the room and shut the door.
Ralph sighed. "You've just met Miller, the gym teacher. He's really great, but you have to do what he says or ..." Ralph said no more, but whatever Miller did, it was clearly terrible. "He usually has a whistle when he comes round here, so you know he's on his way."
"Why do the teachers come round here?"
"We have to be in our rooms from five to six-thirty every evening. That's when we do our homework. The teachers come round to make sure we're here and to make sure we don't read comics. Then the teachers come around again at 10 o'clock when it's time for bed. Today is Miller's day, so you get into bed and stay in bed."
"And Mr Clay. What's he like?"
"We don't know. He's new here himself."
Just then Mr Clay and Thomas's mother came in with the rest of his luggage. It landed on his bed with his other bags. His mother looked at her watch.
"I haven't got much more time, Thomas. If you come down with me, we can say goodbye outside."
Thomas nodded and followed her.
"Mr Clay seems to be a very nice man," she said as they walked towards the car. "Remember what he said: if you have any problems, you can always go to him. He has a nice flat at the end of your corridor." She stopped to open the car door. "If you're not happy, you can always phone me."
Then suddenly she took him in her arms. It surprised him because he hadn't expected it. "You know how much I love you, Thomas. You have to stay here because I can't take you with me. And it isn't possible for your father either. It'll soon be holidays and then you'll be able to come and see

me. The school will organize the plane ticket for you. Then we'll have a wonderful time together. Goodbye, Thomas."

She kissed him and climbed into the car. He felt stiff, like a statue as he stood where everybody could see him near the large, silver-grey car. Then the engine started and the car rolled out of the school as quietly as it had entered.

Thomas's heart nearly burst. It thumped in his chest like a fist inside him. He breathed deeply and heavily to stop the tears. She had left him. In a place he hadn't chosen, with people he didn't know.

And then another bell rang, louder almost than all the others, and he was surrounded by noise as pupils ran out of the different houses on their way to the evening meal.

He felt helpless. He looked around, and didn't know which way to go or who to follow, till a voice shouted, "Hey, Thomas. This way."

It was Ralph. He had come out of Warren House and seen him. Thomas followed him, keeping as near as possible to the only person he knew.

Chapter Two

Later that evening John Clay left his flat and walked through the grounds of Hartlands. Everything was quiet and peaceful. Darkness had arrived and the lights along the paths and in the different buildings made the school feel warm and comfortable. He walked slowly, said hallo to those people he recognized, and thought, Hartlands really is a beautiful place. The old buildings stood separately in their own grounds with gardens, flowers and trees. He wondered what the place had been in earlier times, a rich man's country home or had it belonged to the church? Whether men of the world or men of God, the rich certainly knew where to build their homes. And now it was a school, although still home to the rich. In some of the buildings were the pupils' rooms, in others the different classrooms. Then there were offices, a dining-room, a modern gym and swimming-pool, workshops and rooms for all kinds of activities. Nobody should be bored in Hartlands, he thought. And nobody should really be unhappy.

After a long walk he went back to his flat and opened the living-room window. From here he listened to the sounds of the evening. Hartlands was an oasis of peace and beauty in the English countryside. Less than a mile away on the other side of the trees, cars and heavy lorries thundered along the main roads, while the busy railway lines carried their passengers and commuters into London. They were so close, yet so far away. This was a place where he could stay, Clay thought.

At 10 o'clock the peace and calm were suddenly over. Pupils ran shouting in and out of their rooms; toilets flushed; water taps ran, doors banged open and shut. And over and above all this noise Clay heard a whistle and a sharp military voice shouted, "McGuire, into bed. Smith, turn the radio off."

Clay shut the window and listened carefully. Again the whistle. Again the commands. And in a very short time – silence. Clay walked towards his door, which led to the dormitory. Experience had taught him that whoever was out there had authority, and anybody with that kind of authority was somebody he should know.

He stepped out into the corridor. It was empty and in almost complete darkness. Only one light burned at the end near the stairs to the Lower Dormitory. Nobody was moving, nobody was talking or making any noise. Clay stood still in the dark corridor. Under the doors he could see lights where some pupils were still awake and reading. Then suddenly a door opened and the light shone across the floor of the corridor. But before Clay could say anything, that same military voice barked out of the darkness. "Gregory, back to bed."

The pupil shot back immediately, shut the door and switched off the light. In other rooms the lights went out and radios were turned down.

"I think everything will be all right now," said the voice from the darkness.

Good God, thought Clay.

"Yes," he said. "I'll keep an eye on things now for a while. Good night."

"Good night," said the voice and a short but powerfully built figure moved out of the darkness into the light above the stairs and without a further word went down to the Lower Dormitory.

John Clay went back into his flat. Not a sound came from the dormitory for the next half hour. Then at 11 o'clock the telephone rang. He sighed and answered it.

"Yes?" he asked.

It was Mrs Winterton. "Mr Graham mentioned this evening that you had moved into the flat in the Upper Dormitory, Mr Morrison's old flat."

"That's right," said Clay.

"I'm so glad," she said in a very nice kind voice.

"Thank you," said Clay.

"I'm sure you are the right person." She paused and Clay wondered what she wanted. "Would you be good enough to look into one of the rooms in the Lower Dormitory, please, where the older boys are? One of the windows is open and a terrible noise is coming out. It is 11 o'clock. Really the boys should be asleep by now."

"I'm not really responsible for the Lower Dormitory," Clay said. "My flat is in the Upper Dormitory."

"I'm sure it is," she said. "But Mr Miller, who lives below you, is probably in bed. He's not as young as he used to be."

Clay sighed. "I'll look into it."

He put down the phone and started to leave the flat. Time to play the policeman, he thought.

As soon as he opened the door, the long dark corridor lay before him. He realized that in the brightness of his flat he had forgotten all about it. But there it was, a long dark tunnel that he had to walk along, past the dark shadows of those huge wardrobes, towards the one light at the top of the stairs. It was frightening; it was a no-man's land that you didn't enter unless you had to. Like a forest, you left it to the animals that moved around during the hours of darkness, and stayed where you were safe until the morning. Clay walked towards the light and went quietly down the stairs to the Lower Dormitory.

It was exactly the same as the Upper Dormitory: the same wardrobes, the same doors, the same lights, the same dark brown colours. He stopped outside the room where the noise was and tried to open the door. It was locked. He knocked loudly and waited.

Nothing happened.

He knocked again, louder. A voice called, "Who is it?"

"Clay," he said. He started to feel nervous. The key turned, but nobody opened the door. Clay pushed against it. It opened a few inches and banged against a chair. Angrily Clay pushed the door as hard as he could and a voice shouted, "Wait a minute." He pushed further. Chairs moved and voices started to complain as the door opened. Clay switched on the light and found himself opposite a group of older pupils. The room stank of cigarettes. And on a shelf a colour television was showing a late night film.

A pupil who was standing behind Clay pushed the door. It shut noisily. Clay felt himself shrink. He was suddenly a man among men.

Clay looked around. "Mrs Winterton has complained that you're making too much noise. The others can't sleep."

They laughed. Not aggressively. They just thought it was funny that Mrs Winterton and half of Hartlands couldn't sleep. "I'm sorry," said Clay. "I don't make the rules here. I can only do my job. And you should be quiet after 10 o'clock."

"You don't honestly expect us to go to bed at 10 o'clock," said one of the pupils. He was tall, strong and had blond hair. He was obviously one of the school's athletes.

"I didn't say anything about bed," said Clay, trying to control his anger. "I said you're supposed to be quiet. Some people may want to go to bed at 10 o'clock, and surely nobody should stop them."

"They can go to bed. We're not stopping them," said a pupil in the corner.

"You're making a noise."

"We're watching a film on TV," said another boy. "It doesn't finish till 12.30."

"Look," said Clay. "If you turn the TV down and shut the windows, then you can watch it till tomorrow morning."

"You can't breathe if we shut the windows. The air gets really bad."

"Well, don't smoke," he said loudly. "You're not allowed to smoke in your rooms."

"That's an interesting point," said the boy with the blond hair. "Let's discuss it."

"There's nothing to discuss," said Clay.

"We always discuss things," said the same pupil. "Since Mr Graham has been headmaster here, we discuss everything."

Clay looked straight at the pupil with the blond hair. He was sitting in a dark corner of the room, smiling confidently. "You heard what I said. You're not allowed to smoke in your rooms. You know that very well."

"Some of us are 18."

"What's that got to do with it? It still isn't allowed if you're 80."

One pupil laughed. "Have we got anybody here who is 80 ?"

Suddenly the door flew open and a sharp military voice said, "Bradley, go to my room and wait for me. I'll see you in five minutes. Kelly, Dixon, Webb, rooms. Quickly." And then loudly: "I said quickly. What's taking you so long? Move!"

The boys began to leave the room quickly. "Yes, sir. Sorry, sir," they said as they went past. The last to leave was Bradley. He looked straight into Clay's eyes, smiled, but said nothing.

Clay turned to the teacher whose voice he had now heard twice in one evening and whose authority he envied. He was surprised. The man was short and much older than Clay had imagined, at least 60. But he was clearly strong and clearly fit for his age. "Thank you," said Clay.

The man nodded. "It's all right. You just need a little time, that's all. Believe me, I know them. You'll be all right."

"A little time," said Clay. "How long?"

"I've been here 40 years," he said, as if that was his answer. "You'll be all right. The other teacher. What was his name – Morrison. He was no good. But you'll be all right."

They came to the older man's flat. It was below Clay's. So this was Miller, the man who wasn't as young as he used to be. But when Miller appeared, everybody ran.

Bradley was already standing outside Miller's door. Miller didn't even look at him. He took out his key and said, "Tomorrow at two o'clock. You can help me to paint the fences round the tennis court." He entered his flat and left Clay and the pupil outside.
"Goodnight, Mr Clay," said Bradley and walked away down the dark corridor to his room. He moved confidently and easily. Clay could imagine him on the beach in summer, or in winter on his skis, the centre of attraction, surrounded by friends and girls. He had shown Clay already that respect was not one of his strong points.
"Goodnight," said Clay and climbed the stairs to his flat. He was tired, but the events of the night were not yet over.

* * *

It was after midnight. The dormitory was quiet and dark. Only the one light burned at the far end near the top of the stairs. Two older pupils came up those stairs slowly from below. They were excited and laughed quietly as they moved from step to step. They were carrying a large plastic sack. As they came under the light at the top of the stairs, you could see that one of them was tall with blond hair, but before you could see more, they had left the light and were in the darkness of the dormitory.
They moved slowly and quietly towards the washrooms. There they turned on one of the taps and began to fill the sack with water. When it was half full, they turned off the tap and left the room, pulling the sack along the ground behind them. They moved from door to door and checked the names as they walked along. When they came to number 12, they stopped. The names on the door said Ralph Jenkins and Thomas Walker.
The pupil with the blond hair stood back and then suddenly kicked the door hard. As it flew open, they ran in and threw the sack of water onto the boy in the nearest bed.

Thomas screamed as soon as he felt the cold water, and the sack fell on top of him.

"Welcome to Hartlands!" shouted one of the boys and together they ran out of the room and back down the dark corridor before the others could get out of bed or switch on the lights.

Ralph was awake immediately. He jumped over the wet floor and out of the door into the dark corridor in time to see the two older boys as they ran down the stairs to the Lower Dormitory. In other rooms lights were also switched on and here and there a door opened as a head looked out and sleepily asked what had happened.

"It's all right," said Ralph helplessly. "Thomas got the treatment."

Ralph went back into the room. Thomas was sitting up in bed. He was frightened and in a state of shock. His pyjamas were wet, his bed was wet, and water was all over the floor. Ralph took all the towels he could find and threw them on the floor. Then he took his keys out of his trousers and went to his wardrobe outside in the corridor. He took out a sleeping bag and gave it to Thomas.

"Here," he said. "Use this till morning."

Thomas nodded and climbed out of bed. Together they pulled the blankets away and threw them onto the floor in the water. Ralph tested the mattress; it was wet, so they turned it over.

"You'll be all right now if you dry yourself."

"Will they come back?" asked Thomas.

"No, it won't happen again."

But Thomas still looked shocked and frightened.

"Don't worry," said Ralph. "It's happened to all of us."

He pushed the broken door until it was almost shut and put their desk against it, so that nobody could get in without making a noise. Then he went back to his bed and switched off the light. Soon he was asleep again.

In the sleeping bag, Thomas lay awake for a long time. He listened to the sounds of the old building as it rested through the night. Tears were in his eyes and he felt very, very lonely. His mother was a long way away, and he was here without a family. He would run away immediately – if only he knew where he could go.

In his flat at the end of the dormitory John Clay slept on. He had no idea what had happened.

Chapter Three

The dining-room was, as always, noisy. What made it so noisy, Clay thought, was the fact that the room was so large and the ceiling so high. The noise of two hundred plates, all the knives and forks, echoed around the walls. You couldn't hear words, you couldn't hear conversations, you could only hear noise. Until you heard the gong. The gong was the signal that the meal was over. Then the noise got less and less until the room was quiet. So it was every day. And so it was today. The gong rang, Mr Graham, the headmaster, stood up and waited until the very last person had finally stopped talking. Then he spoke loudly and clearly. What he had to say was for everybody in the room.

"It seems that the old tradition of throwing water over new pupils in the middle of the night has started again."

Some pupils laughed, many cheered.

"I do not find this funny," he said angrily. At once the room was quiet. "I am sure we can find a better way of welcoming pupils to Hartlands." He waited while he watched the faces to see who was still laughing, who was listening.

"I thought we had agreed at our last pupil-teacher meeting," he said more seriously, "that this stupid and dangerous tradition should stop. If I remember correctly, the majority of you agreed that it should stop. But clearly, some of you don't respect the opinion of the majority. I said then, and I will say it again, such action as throwing water onto a sleeping person can have serious consequences. The shock can be so great that the pupil could, for example, have a heart attack."

At the mention of a heart attack, those pupils who had been looking dreamily out of the windows or looking at the walls in front of them, came awake. Several laughed. Others looked around. Heart attack? Heart attack? Who has had a heart attack? Thomas, knowing that he was that person, went red. From the next table he heard a voice say, "Where is this cripple with a weak heart?"

John Clay heard the question, too. He pressed his lips together and sat quietly at his table. He saw the sadness in Thomas's eyes and felt very sorry for him.

"Furthermore," said Mr Graham, "the door was kicked in, another sign that brutality is coming back into the daily life of this school. It must stop."

"If he's stupid enough to lock it," somebody whispered, "what does he expect?"

Clay looked around more carefully, studied the faces. At one table a group of pupils was trying not to laugh. But one of them was grinning openly. Clay recognized the blond hair at once. It was the pupil he had seen outside Miller's flat the night before. He thought hard, but the pupil's name escaped him.

"You all know our system," said Mr Graham. "I expect those of you who did this to excuse themselves and pay for the repairs."

The headmaster paused and waited for a reaction. Nobody moved or raised a hand. The teachers looked from table to table, from face to face. The pupils glanced only at each other.

"I have tried to create a system here," said Mr Graham, "that is based on fairness. I have suggested rules that we can all agree to, rules which should make our lives here together more comfortable. And I expect fairness from *everybody*. Throwing water over new pupils is not in our rules."

Mr Graham paused again for a second time, but still there was no reaction. The whole school sat patiently and waited.

"I have said before," he said more loudly than ever, "that our community is built on laws which all of us can and must accept. Unfortunately, if we are not careful, it will be destroyed by the lawlessness of a few individuals."

Mr Graham looked around the room. Nobody wanted to say who had done it. It had happened and a new day could start.

"I will be in my office all afternoon," said Mr Graham. "If the person who did this wants to come to me, he can find me there. But first I wish to see the following boys from the Lower Dormitory now after lunch: Henderson, Mathews, Kelly and Drew." There were protests at once. "It's football practice, sir."

"I don't care what it is," said Mr Graham. "I wish to know who did this, football practice or not. Any more announcements?" He asked this last question in a more relaxed voice and a pupil from Clay's table stood up.

"The workshop will be open all afternoon and until 10 o'clock tonight."

He sat down again, while another boy stood up.

"There'll be no pottery this afternoon. Mrs Webb is ill."

Mr Graham looked around. Nobody else stood up.

"Letters," he said.

A pupil began to read from a list of names. On the table next to him were a number of letters. After the names had been read, Mr Graham left the table and walked out of the room. Slowly the teachers and pupils stood up and followed him. Those pupils whose names had been read out stood in a line to receive their letters.

* * *

Outside, John Clay stopped Peter Hansen, the German teacher. He was a younger man like himself, but he had already been at Hartlands almost two years.

"Does the name Brad mean anything to you?" he asked.

Peter Hansen stopped on the path as the pupils hurried past them, some to their rooms, others to the sports field.

"Brad?" he asked curiously. "Where did you get that name?"

"Thomas's room-mate mentioned it."

Peter Hansen whistled softly to himself. "Well, well, well." He looked around into the faces of the pupils as they came out of the room.

"Ralph, come here, please," he called suddenly.

Ralph freed himself from a group of pupils and walked over to the two teachers.

"All right," said Hansen. "Who was it?"

"It was dark," said Ralph nervously. "I couldn't see properly."

"You said it was Brad."

Ralph looked away towards his friends, who were waiting for him. "I told Thomas it could have been Brad," he said. "He's done it before. I didn't know Thomas would run straight to Mr Clay."

"Oh, yes? When was this?"

"I don't know. You just hear things."

"Tell me some of the things you've heard. Perhaps I'm interested."

"It was before Mr Graham came. When we had the old head. It happened to all the new pupils."

"Is Brad back to his old tricks, Ralph?"

"I don't know. I mean ... I mean, it was too dark to tell. It could have been him."

"Okay," said Hansen. "You can go. But why don't you come and see me later this afternoon and bring Thomas with you?"

"All right," said Ralph and ran back to his friends. The two teachers just heard the short report. "Got to see Hansen this afternoon. Don't know why."

They continued along the path towards Warren House.

"Who is this Brad?" said Clay. "If it's the person I'm thinking of, he's got blond hair. Is that right?"

Hansen didn't reply at once. Instead he looked at the ground as they walked slowly away from the dining-room. "He's possibly the worst pupil we've got," he said.

"I've been trying to catch him for over a year, but I can't lay a finger on him. Somebody always covers up for him, and I've never found out why." They paused outside Warren House.

"Just like today," said Hansen. "Nobody will say that it was Brad." He ran his hand through his hair. "So what do you do? He has got his claws into everybody and everything that is going on here. He's like a cancer that is working its way through the whole school and all you can do is watch."

"Why doesn't the head throw him out?"

"Because nobody can prove anything. Also, Bradley can be very nice and very charming. And he's always very nice to Mr Graham."

"And to the other teachers?"

"The only person he's frightened of is Miller, the sports teacher. But Brad is one of Miller's best sportsmen, so there's not much hope there. And he's quite strong."

Clay nodded. "I was surprised for such an old man."

Hansen smiled. "I don't mean Miller. I mean Brad."

"I see." Clay breathed in. "This place gets less like paradise every day."

Hansen laughed. "I wouldn't worry. You look fit enough. Brad might be a bit more careful with you. Word has already got out that you're not a softie. But they'll test you a little more before they've made up their minds."

Clay suddenly remembered the look in Brad's face as he had walked past him in the room in the dormitory and then again as he had left him outside Miller's room.

A group of younger pupils ran towards Clay and Hansen.

"What do you lot want?" asked Hansen.

"We wanted to ask Mr Clay if he'll play rugby with us."

Hansen laughed loudly. "This is it, John. The next test. I wouldn't do it. If they get you on the ground, that's it." He laughed and shook his head.

"Will you play with us, sir?" shouted one of the boys. "Just for half an hour."

Clay looked at Hansen, but Hansen just shook his head again and walked away. "You're on your own."

"OK," said Clay. "I'll be along in a minute. Where are you?"

"On the sports field."

Hansen shouted back, "I'll be in the workshop. I'll tell them to prepare a coffin for you."

Chapter Four

Hartlands had a pub. Not a real pub, of course, like in the town, but the pupils called it "the Pub", and they liked to think of it as their own special room where they were allowed to be alone and play music, or sit and talk with friends. It was open every evening from seven till 10 o'clock. It had a proper bar with tables and chairs, and behind the bar were barmen who served drinks to the pupils. Only – the drinks were non-alcoholic.

John Clay was shocked when he walked into the dark room for the first time, more by accident than by intention.

"What'll it be, Mr Clay?" asked the barman for that evening, a pupil from one of his A-level English classes.

Clay looked around; he still couldn't quite believe his eyes. "What?"

"What'll it be?" the barman repeated. "Beer?"

"Beer?" said Clay. "You have beer here? Does Mr Graham know that?"

"We keep a bottle now and again for special guests."

The barman took a bottle out of a fridge and opened it before Clay could say yes or no to the offer. Clay accepted the glass and as his eyes got used to the darkness, he noticed other pupils in the room.

"Not bad," he said. "How long have you had this?"

"About 10 months," said the barman. "The idea is to stop us leaving the school in the evening and going into town to get drunk."

"So you get drunk here instead?"

"No, of course not. We're only allowed to sell soft drinks. But it's warm and not as far as into town."

"It's the best room in school," said one of the pupils further down the bar. "But the head might shut it again."

"Why's that?" asked Clay.

"He doesn't like the way it's organized," said the barman.

"How is it organized?"

"That's what the head would like to know," said a pupil at the bar.

"Perhaps he ought to ask Brad," said another, and their friends laughed as if it was a school joke.

Clay put his glass down. Suddenly that name was there again. "Brad? What has he got to do with it?"

"He organizes most things. He buys the drinks, decides what the prices should be, chooses the barmen. It means that we can earn some extra pocket-money."

Clay couldn't believe it. "You mean that Brad is running a private business here in the school?"

"Not really. It's the pupils' pub, but, well, he does most of the organization. Somebody has to do it. "

"And Mr Graham allows this?"

Clay looked from face to face, but nobody said anything.

Clay looked around. "Is Brad here?"

The barman shook his head. "Not tonight. I don't know where he is. He'll probably be in later to check the money and pay us."

Clay emptied his glass. "If you've got beer in that fridge for special guests, then there's probably more than one bottle, and I would also guess that some of your special guests aren't teachers."

The pupil said nothing.

"Am I right?" asked Clay.

The pupil started to wash some glasses as if he hadn't heard anything.

"Make sure there's no beer in that fridge when I come here again."

"OK, Mr Clay."

Clay walked out of the pub. Brad, he thought, everywhere he turned he heard the name Brad. He wondered where he was at that moment.

* * *

Brad was, in fact, in the Upper Dormitory. Together with his friend Dexter and two other pupils he was planning to visit Thomas Walker. Gently he knocked on the door, then tried to open it, but it was locked.

"Thomas," he called.

"Who is it?"

Brad knocked again and said, "Come on, Thomas. Open the door."

"What do you want?"

"We'll tell you when we're inside. Now be a good boy and open the door, or do we have to walk through it?"

Inside the room, Thomas sighed helplessly, and began to unlock the door. Brad and his friends walked in, smiling – and threatening.

"Happy birthday, Thomas," said Brad.

"Happy birthday," said the others. And Thomas prepared himself for a catastrophe.

"Why don't you have a party, Thomas?" asked Brad. "Other people have parties when it's their birthday. Why are you sitting here alone?"

"I was going to ..."

"Oh, I see," said Brad. "You were going to celebrate alone."

"No ...," said Thomas, not knowing what to say. Not knowing what would happen if he said the wrong thing.

Dexter started to open cupboards and drawers. "I hear you've got some very nice Swiss chocolates, Thomas?" he asked. "Don't you want to share them with us?"

"They're a present from my mother," said Thomas nervously, watching the boys move around the room.

"That's very kind of her," said Brad. "But why didn't you tell us? Why didn't you invite us? I don't remember that you ever invited us."

Dexter opened another cupboard. Ritchie looked under the bed. A further pupil looked behind the books and in boxes. Somebody else started to open a suitcase.

"Leave my things alone," said Thomas angrily. He tried to take the suitcase from the boy's hands, but the other boy was stronger. Brad moved across and took Thomas's arm. "You're not going to get physical, are you, Thomas?" He took the suitcase and threw it on the bed. "You're not going to try and throw us out, are you?" he asked.

He opened the case and looked inside. "Well, what have we got here?" he asked and took out a large box of chocolates. "These look really good." Thomas felt weak and frustrated. "Leave them alone, please. I told you. They're from my mother."

"Have you got any more of these hidden in here, Thomas?" And the pupils started to break up his room.

A pupil finally found Clay in the library, where he was reading a magazine.

"Mr Clay," he shouted quickly.

"What's wrong?" said Clay.

The pupil was breathing hard; he had run all over the school to find Clay. "Can you go to Thomas Walker's room, please? I think there's a fight in his room."

Clay threw his magazine on the table and left the room. He ran across the grounds and into Warren House. He hurried up the stairs, two at a time, until he came to the Upper Dormitory. The corridor was empty and dark, but he could clearly hear noises from one of the rooms.

He walked down the long corridor until he came to number 12. At the same time he heard a shelf fall over and somebody laughed.

Clay knocked loudly on the door. "Open up!" he shouted. The room fell silent.

"Open this door at once!" shouted Clay and began to feel nervous as he thought who might be in there.

Inside a voice said quietly, "It's Clay. That's all we needed."

Brad turned to Thomas. "OK, Thomas, start cleaning the room. Dexter, open the door."

Dexter turned the key and Clay pushed his way into the room. The door banged into Dexter's face and pushed him back against the wall.

"Hey, careful," said Dexter.

"Shut up," said Clay.

He looked around the room. Books were on the floor, clothes were all over the bed, cupboards were open.

"What's going on here?" he asked angrily.

"We're celebrating Thomas's birthday, that's all," said Dexter.

"I'm not celebrating anything," said Thomas. "They just came in and started wrecking the room."

"What for?" asked Clay. "I said, what for? Are you all deaf?"

"It's his birthday," said Ritchie.

"Oh, it's his birthday. So you come in here and start wrecking the room."

The boys stood quietly in a group in the middle of the room. While Clay faced them, Thomas started to pick up books and put them back on the shelves.

"Well, don't just stand there!" said Clay loudly. "Help him and then get out."

Nobody moved.

"I said help him," Clay repeated.

"He can do it himself," said Dexter. "He's a mother's boy ..."

Clay turned to Dexter.

"Pick those books up."

Dexter sighed and very slowly picked up a book. He stood there with it in his hand. "Where do you want it, Thomas?" he asked with a bored voice.

Clay pushed him violently across the room. His face was white with anger. He was almost trembling as he said, "Try the bookshelf. That's what they're usually for."

Dexter turned round quickly. "Don't push me," he said. "There's a law ..."

But suddenly Brad stepped forward. "Come on, let's do as Mr Clay says. Let's help Thomas." He bent down and picked up several books.

The others obeyed, almost relieved that they could move.

"It's all right," said Thomas. "I'd prefer to do it myself. They'll only put everything in the wrong place."

"Are you sure?" asked Clay.

Thomas nodded. "I know where everything goes."

"OK," said Clay. "The rest of you get out."

Brad placed the books he was holding very gently on the desk.

"I think we ought to go," he said. "Teacher seems to be angry."

"Bradley."

Brad stopped. "Mr Clay?"

"I can do without those comments."

"Comments? What comments?" He looked at Clay. " You should try not to lose control of yourself too much," he said politely. "It damages relations between teachers and pupils."

"Get out," said Clay.

Brad smiled warmly, politely said goodnight and led the pupils out of the room. As he walked out, Brad passed Clay so closely that their two bodies almost touched. Again Brad looked straight into Clay's eyes. Again there was a smile on his lips.

Clay watched them walk out. Once they had left and the door shut again, he slowly began to relax. Then he looked around the room.

"I'll help you to clean up, Thomas. It'll be quicker then."

"No, really. I'd prefer to do it myself."

Clay sat on the side of the bed. "You're not very happy here, are you, Thomas?"

Thomas paused, then he laughed cynically. "You've seen what happens. You try and have a nice room and nice things around you and they come and wreck everything."

"Have you got any friends here?"

Thomas nodded. "But not Brad and Dexter."

Clay waited for a few seconds before he asked his next question.

"Why did you come to Hartlands?"

"My parents are divorced," he said. "My father travels a lot and ... my mother lives in Switzerland." Suddenly he smiled warmly. "I might be able to see her during the holidays. She said in her last letter I might be able to go and live with her. Have you ever been to Switzerland?"

Clay nodded. "It's a nice country." Clay stood up. "It'll be nice to go to your mother, Thomas. But don't run away from here. Are you sure I can't help you?"

Thomas shook his head. "I'll finish the rest tomorrow. Thanks all the same."

"OK. I'll go back now." Clay paused, seemed to think for a while before he said, "Goodnight, Thomas."

Thomas had already sat down at his desk. "Goodnight, Mr Clay."

Clay opened the door and stepped into the dark unfriendly corridor. In both directions he could see only a long line of large brown cupboards and between them brown doors. Even the walls and ceilings were brown. He was right. Colour was missing. But even if they painted it red, white and blue, the colours couldn't hide the loneliness inside the small rooms, the loneliness of young people far away from home. At that moment Hartlands no longer seemed to be the paradise he had imagined. It had become a cold and cruel place, a place where only cold and cruel people could survive. Clay opened the door to Thomas's room again. Thomas was still sitting at his desk, putting a new battery into a small radio.

"If you like," said Clay nervously. "If you don't want to sit alone in your room, you can always come to my flat. I've got a television. You can always come and watch it."

Thomas smiled, grateful for the offer. "Really? That would be very nice. Thanks a lot."

Clay nodded and before Thomas could say anything else, he backed out of the room and shut the door.

Slowly Clay walked along the empty corridor to his flat. Before he put the key in the lock he looked down to the far end where the stairs led to the Lower Dormitory. A pupil came up the stairs and appeared in the unclear light. Clay recognized the blond hair at once. Bradley. He watched more closely to see where the pupil was going, but Brad had seen him, too. Brad knocked on a door and walked into a room. It wasn't Thomas's room.

Clay opened his door and entered his flat.

Chapter Five

Peter Hansen walked into Clay's flat and said, "I like it."

John Clay looked at the half-empty room. "How can you say you like this? I haven't been here long enough to buy any furniture. I borrowed all this from the school."

"Not your flat," said Hansen. "Your new name. Killer Clay. It's good. I like it."

Clay offered Hansen a cup of tea and invited him to sit down in the only comfortable chair in the room.

"So you've heard."

"Everybody has heard," said Hansen. He laughed loudly and drank from his tea. "It's a good start. Keep going like that and you'll have no problems in Hartlands. Where's the sugar?"

"You'll have to drink it without. I forgot to buy some." Then Clay sighed and sat down at his desk. "I suppose they all ran to the head and told him."

Hansen shrugged. "Don't worry. It isn't Mr Graham's idea of education to shout at people and push them around. But if you ask me, it's the only language some of them understand, especially Bradley."

"It didn't seem to impress him."

"It impressed the others, and that's the main thing." Hansen looked at his watch. "You know, John, you make a terrible cup of tea. Let's drive into town. I know a nice little café where you aren't surrounded by Hartlands people."

"Fine," said Clay, and together the two teachers left the flat.

"I was in the school pub last night," said Clay as they walked along the dormitory.

"It's wonderful, isn't it?"

"A pupil said the head wasn't happy with the organization of the place."

"Would you be?"

"Not if it's true what I heard, that Brad runs the place and pays the barmen."

"Exactly. The idea to have a kind of pub in the school was a good idea. It means the pupils have really got a room of their own where they can be together and do what they want. But I've often noticed that people basically are lazy. They're like sheep. You have a good idea, but it stays as an idea because nobody wants to do anything with it. Then somebody like Brad sees that nobody is doing anything and decides to take the idea over. And strangely enough everybody seems to be quite happy."

"So where's the problem? It seems that Brad is a very good businessman."

"Too good. He's making a lot of money. And nobody knows where the money goes to, who gets it or what happens with it."

"Is that why the head wants to shut the pub?"

"Let's say we're going to have an inquiry soon, and Brad will have to explain very clearly where every penny goes. If the head is satisfied, it'll stay open. If, as I suppose, the money goes into Brad's pocket, then that's the end of it. Or at least we'll have to organize it differently."

As they left the building, a large impressive car drove into the school grounds and stopped outside the main office. The man who got out was equally large and impressive, a man who gave orders to others and never took them himself.

"Bradley's father," said Hansen. "Five minutes with him and you can understand his son. It's not very often that we see him here. It must be important."

* * *

It *was* important. Mr Bradley had travelled a long way to visit Hartlands, and the visit was costing him time, time that he could use more usefully for other things. He was serious and determined as he locked the car doors and walked lightly into the office.

"Bradley," he said with a sudden friendly smile. "Mr Richards is expecting me."

Mr Richards was the deputy headmaster. "He's in his office," said the secretary. "I'll tell him that you are here."

"Thank you," said Mr Bradley and walked towards Mr Richards' office before the secretary could lift the phone and say who had arrived.

Mr Bradley knocked on the door and walked in. Mr Richards was answering the phone. He seemed surprised that the door should open but when he saw the visitor, he pointed with his free hand to a large comfortable chair in a corner of the room. Mr Bradley sat down and waited patiently until the conversation was over. Then Mr Richards stood up and came over to his guest.

"It's good to see you again in Hartlands. You're lucky to find me here, or do you have my timetable in your car?"

Mr Bradley enjoyed the joke and smiled warmly.

"Before I forget," continued the deputy head, "let me thank you for the chairs that you sent for our new school theatre."

"I'm glad you liked them. One always tries to do something for one's old school when possible."

"Can I offer you anything? Tea or coffee?"

"Coffee, please," said Mr Bradley and glanced at his watch, as if to say I don't have a lot of time.

Mr Richards understood, gave the order to the secretary and sat down opposite his guest. "Mrs Ellis said you had phoned and wanted to see me, but you didn't say why."

"Let's say Stewart seems to have a problem with his maths."

Mr Richards was surprised. Not only was he the deputy head but he was also Brad's maths teacher. "I don't understand. His last test was good. We went over the work in private lessons, as you wished, and the results were very good."

"I haven't really come here to discuss his lessons or the tests. Stewart said you helped him very much, and I'd like to thank you for that ..."

Just then the secretary came in with the coffee, and Mr Bradley paused while she put the cups and sugar on the table. After she had left the room, he said, "My son has a different problem, which needs a little attention and possibly a little advice. I was hoping you might be able to help me."

Mr Richards sat back with his coffee cup in his hand and listened carefully.

"I believe the headmaster and a certain teacher – Hansen I believe his name is – want to hold a kind of public inquiry into my son's organization of the school pub. By public I mean in front of all the other pupils."

Mr Richards nodded. "A week on Wednesday. In the drama room. It was the headmaster's idea to have it there. An inquiry is full of drama, he believes."

"Is it necessary at all?"

"It can't be stopped. Not now." Mr Richards took off his glasses. He didn't really like Hansen very much, but there were limits to what he could do. "There are a number of problems," he said. "As I understand it from the pupils, the main problem is not the organization of the pub. Most pupils seem quite happy with it and are quite happy that Stewart organizes everything. The problem seems to be the financial side, especially the accounts."

Mr Bradley nodded thoughtfully and drank from his coffee. He placed the cup back on the table carefully. "I see," he said. "I've discussed the whole thing with my son. He tells me that he has invested quite a lot of money in the pub, that he buys the drinks and pays the barmen and that this Hansen believes he is making huge profits. Can that be?"

It was becoming an unpleasant situation for Mr Richards. "Mr Hansen is very interested in how much money Stewart is making in the pub and where that money is going, that is correct. If Stewart could show proper accounts and explain,..." Mr Richards paused, then walked towards a window from where he could see the green lawns of Hartlands. Then he continued, "... how that money was spent, all of it, so that, let's say, there was no profit, or very little profit, then I am sure that Mr Hansen's case would not be very successful. But I am not an accountant."

"I have accountants in the firm," said Mr Bradley. "But," Mr Bradley seemed to think for a short while as though a new idea had come to him. "Why don't you and your wife come and visit us next weekend and we can discuss this more informally? It has been a long time since you and Carol had dinner with us." Before Mr Richards could answer, Mr Bradley added, "Perhaps we could say Saturday at 7.30? Stewart will be at home then."

Mr Richards nodded. "Saturday evening will be fine."

"Good." The two men rose from their seats.

"I'm very grateful that you took the time to see me," said Mr Bradley.

"Have you any plans for your son's future career?" asked Mr Richards as they left the office and walked towards Mr Bradley's car.

"I had thought that he could stay here until he has done his A-levels. I realize that Stewart is not very academic, but if he is to follow me in the firm, I feel he ought to have something on paper."

"I'm sure he'll do very well in the firm," said Mr Richards. "He certainly seems to see the opportunities before the others."

"Well, that's what we need in this country, people who see the opportunities and do something. Is Carol happy with the new kitchen?"

"Oh, very much. The men you sent to install it were very good."

"I only ever send the best – to you, that is."
The two men were now outside in the school grounds. "Tell me, how is our dear headmaster?" asked Mr Bradley, now standing in front of his car.
"Parents still complain. They don't like some of his methods, too much freedom, too little discipline. He changes things and never informs the parents."
"Exactly. It's the parents who finance this school, and I believe they should also decide how it is organized. When old Matthews was here, he was strict and his methods weren't very modern, but it was a school. Good discipline, that's what he had. I don't send my son here to discuss things or learn how to live democratically and fairly with other people. I send him here to learn maths, so that he can pass his exams. And thank God there are still teachers like yourself here who continue the tradition of Hartlands. A number of parents have already said to me, if Graham goes, it's clear who should be the next headmaster."
Bradley unlocked the car and opened the driver's door.
"I hope to see you on Saturday then."
Richards nodded. "See you on Saturday."

Chapter Six

Life at Hartlands had the rhythm of a heartbeat, regular and every day the same routine, so that time passed and you never noticed anything. Until it had happened, and then it was like a shock because it was suddenly so unexpected. John Clay came out of his flat on one such day as pupils were running about everywhere in the dormitory, obviously in a hurry.

"Hey, what's happening?" he asked.

"It's Brad's trial today, Mr Clay. Have you forgotten?"

Clay had indeed forgotten.

"At four o'clock in the drama room. If you want a good seat, sir, you'll have to go early. All the school will be there."

The inquiry into the organization of the school pub and Brad's role in it. That he really wanted to see. Hansen was the prosecutor, pupils and teachers the jury, and the headmaster was the judge. The choice of the drama room was excellent, as this was possibly the best form of drama Hartlands had to offer.

The pupils all came early; they crowded into the room as if they had come to a rock concert or a football match. Excitement filled the air. They cheered when the jury came in and sat at a long table on the stage. They whistled and booed when Peter Hansen took his seat at a separate table and began to look through lots of different papers.

Brad was clearly the favourite and, like a good entertainer, he came last.

He chose his time well. As he left the dormitory, the grounds outside were almost empty. Friends who hadn't gone to the trial shouted, "All the best, Brad."

"Give it to them, Brad," somebody else shouted. "No problem," said Brad. "I'll run rings round them."

As he walked down the path towards the drama room, a younger pupil ran up to him.

"Hey, Brad."

Brad stopped. He recognized the pupil and started to speak to him before the younger boy could continue.

"Next week. OK? I've got other problems at the moment."

The pupil was breathless. "But Brad. You promised. You said you'd give me the papers this week."

"I've not had a chance to go home yet. Look, I'll have them next week. OK?"

He started to walk away, but the pupil ran after him. "Hansen said ..."

Brad stopped immediately. "Hansen? What's he got to do with it. You leave Hansen out of this. Do you hear me?"

"He said I had to tax and insure the bike or he would take it away from me."

"Hansen can go to hell," said Brad violently. "You'll get your papers. Now leave me alone."

He turned round and walked angrily away from the pupil. The boy stood sadly alone for a minute, then he too turned and walked back to the dormitory.

* * *

The drama room was full, and the noise seemed to get louder and louder as the crowd waited for their hero to appear. Mr Graham, the headmaster, banged on his table with a small hammer and decided to talk to the pupils before the main event started.

"We have come together today to look at the organization of the school pub. The pub was created for the use of all pupils. It is a room where pupils can meet. It is not, and I repeat, it is not a private business for one or two individuals."

At that moment the door opened and Brad walked in. He smiled and lifted his arms. The crowd had their star. Some cheered, others whistled. The drama could begin.

Brad jumped lightly onto the stage and sat down at a table that had been prepared for him. He was neatly dressed.

Confidently he opened his briefcase and took out a number of papers. He looked through them professionally, while the pupils in the crowd below got ready for the show of the year.

Peter Hansen stood up. "OK, Brad. We'll go through the points one by one. We'll make it simple so that even the least intelligent can understand."

Brad nodded as if to say, I agree.

"You buy your drinks for – let us say X pence a bottle. You sell them in the pub for Y pence a bottle. That is normal business."

Brad nodded.

"The difference is what we call profit. The problem here is that the difference between the price you pay for the drinks and the price for which you sell is exactly 100%. That is a lot of money. And if we think of how many crates of drinks you sell every week, then we are not talking about £10 or even £20. We are talking about hundreds of pounds. And I'd like to know where that money goes."

The room was suddenly silent. Nobody had ever really thought how much money Brad was making in the pub. Suddenly it became serious.

Brad smiled. "Firstly, the difference between the price I pay for the drinks and the price I sell them for is not my profit. As you know, Mr Hansen, every business has expenses. My profit comes *after* all the expenses. The question we really want to ask is whether I have any profit at all. And what you have also forgotten is the price of drinks in the pub is cheaper than anywhere else in town."

That was true. The audience cheered and whistled. Brad was in front on points.

Hansen was not impressed. "Expenses? What expenses? The school gives you the room. You don't pay rent, you don't pay electricity. You didn't even pay for the furniture. One of the parents supplied that. The school even decorated the room. You'll have to think of something better than that. I don't see any expenses. Where are they?"

The crowd cheered again. It was a good fight and even Hansen had earned some support. The circus was in full swing.

"Firstly," said Brad, "I have to organize when the drinks are delivered and make sure somebody is here to unload them. I usually pay the people who help us. Then I don't ask for a deposit on the bottles. If a pupil breaks the bottle or takes it away, I have to pay for that bottle."

"Pupils aren't allowed to take bottles out of the pub."

"They aren't allowed to do a lot of things in this school, but they still do them," said Brad. "I only sell the drinks. If I start to check what they do with them, then I'll have to pay for a doorman. That means more expenses."

That brought more cheers from the audience. "I also have to pay pupils who work behind the bar. Then we have damage. Things always get broken, glasses, mirrors."

"Most of them were stolen in the first place," shouted a pupil from the audience.

"Last week somebody broke a window..."

"Pupils are insured against damage," said Peter Hansen. "Why didn't you claim it from their insurance?"

"Nobody saw who it was. So I have to pay for it. This goes on all the time. Then what about all the decorations, the lights, the cassette-recorder, record-player and records? The pupils want music. At first I used my own record- player, my own records. And what happened? Everything is ruined. I haven't got one record without a scratch. And those are *my* records. And you talk of profit."

"Even if we accept these small costs, your profit is huge."

"What profit?" Brad interrupted Hansen. "Anybody would think the pub has made me a millionaire."

"It has," shouted another pupil from the audience. Others laughed.

"You won't believe this, but I've probably put more into the pub than I've got out of it. I pay the barmen; I pay if things get broken. I run around to buy drinks. And what happens if nobody comes? Nobody ever asks that question. Then I've got crates and crates of drinks – crates that I've paid for. I've got to carry all the risks – and I'm still a criminal?"

"Don't tell me you're doing this out of the kindness of your heart or for the love of your fellow pupils. The pub is a non-profit making organization for the pupils."

"That's right," said Brad. "Whenever we have had a good month, then we have a free drinks evening."

"They're only for your friends," shouted a pupil. "Nobody else gets a drink."

"That is nonsense," said Brad angrily. "Free drinks are free drinks – for everybody. But if the pub is full, it's full and I have to shut the door. We have fire regulations here. I can't let two hundred pupils come into that room. If you come too late, you're too late. That's it."

Pupils in the audience started to shout back angrily, but Mr Graham put up his hand. Slowly the room became quiet again.

"Let's get to the point," said Hansen. "Expenses, lost bottles, broken windows. This is nothing. This whole conversation is a farce. We are talking about a sum of money which is spent in that pub, money which you collect every evening and nobody knows what happens to it. Nobody even knows exactly how much it is, because there are no receipts, there are no books. There is nothing except excuses and stories."

Brad jumped to his feet. "That is not true. I don't know where you got your information from so far, but that is wrong." He opened his case and took out some documents. "Here, Mr Hansen, are my books. If you want to look at them, you'll soon see that after my expenses, there is hardly any profit at all, certainly not enough to make me a millionaire. If anybody else wants to have the pub, they can.

They'll soon see how much work it is. And we'll soon see if anybody is driving around in a big new car."

Peter Hansen walked quickly across the stage while the pupils whistled and cheered and banged their feet on the floor.

"Where did you get these?" he asked quietly. "You didn't have them last week."

Brad looked up at him confidently. Behind them the pupils were shouting and whistling. The whole room had the atmosphere of a football match.

"I've got them now," he said. "That's the main thing."

Brad stood up and started to put his documents back into his case while Mr Graham banged his little hammer on the table.

"Who did this for you?" said Hansen coldly. "You never did this yourself. You can't count past 10."

Brad looked straight into Hansen's eyes. "Like I said, I've got them. You're welcome to check them." Hansen pressed his teeth together, then shut the book and threw it on the table. As he turned round, his eyes met Mr Richards', but the deputy head looked away. Hansen returned to his seat. In his anger he no longer heard the noise in the room or Mr Graham, as he banged on his table until it was quiet enough for him to talk.

"Attention, please. This is and should remain a democratic discussion about an organization that interests all of us. It is not a football match." Slowly the room became quiet again. "We have just now learned that the books are here. They will be checked by our maths department to see that they are correct." Peter Hansen looked up. When he heard the word maths department, his eyes went thoughtfully over the faces in the audience and again came to Mr Richards, but the deputy head was listening carefully to Mr Graham's words.

"For the future," continued the headmaster, "I suggest that a committee of teachers and pupils discusses together the organization of the pub – the paper work and the expenses, etc. These should also choose a group of, let us say, "Pubsters". By "Pubster" I mean pupils who will do the practical work of organizing the bar and serving the drinks. At the end of every evening a member of staff and a pupil from the committee could then come in and check the money and control the number of drinks that have been sold."

Mr Graham smiled and looked into the audience below him. They were all talking excitedly with each other, exchanging ideas, discussing who was better and who was right or wrong. "Would any pupils like to be members of the new committee. If they could raise their hands?"

Nobody reacted.

Mr Graham looked towards his teachers. Two of them raised their hands.

"Mr Williams and Mrs French. Thank you. And from the pupils?"

From the back of the room two older pupils raised their hands.

"Thank you," said the headmaster. "Perhaps we could meet in my office tomorrow morning."

He rose from his table as if to say the inquiry was over, and at that moment everybody in the room jumped up and tried to get out.

* * *

Two of the last people to leave the room were Brad and Hansen. In the large empty room they stood opposite each other like two men who now knew that they were enemies. There was nothing to hide and no reason to pretend. Brad was still confident. "Bad luck," he said casually as he put his papers and documents into his case. "You tried hard, but, that's the way it goes." He smiled, but Hansen showed no reaction. "You're going to make a mistake one day," said Hansen. "And I'll be there. And do you know what I'll say? OK, Brad, let's talk to Mr Graham, and after that you can pack your cases. I'll drive you to the station myself."

The teacher left his table, his eyes were not even looking at the few pupils who were still standing around, and he walked out of the room.

Brad walked over to his friends. As soon as he stood together with them, the smile left his face and he became more serious. "Find out who opened his mouth. Hansen must have got his information from somebody. He was too well informed."

"Sure," said Dexter. "But what do we do now? The pub was a good business."

"It's finished. You heard what Graham said. There's no money in it now with this committee and all the checks. Anyway we've already got our money out of it, although I still don't have enough for the car I want."

"Ask your father," said Sandy.

"You don't know what he's like. You can't get a penny out of him."

"We could start selling drinks in the evening after lights out."

"That's no good. We need something that brings a quick profit."

"How about ice-cream?" asked Dexter.

"Don't be stupid," said Sandy. "You need a fridge."

"We can always get a used one."

"And where are you going to put it?" said Brad angrily.

"In my room. I'll throw out my desk. I never use it anyway."

"I've got another idea," said Brad as the small group of boys left the drama room.

"What is it?" asked Dexter.

Brad said one word that only Dexter could hear.
"We can't do that," said Dexter. "It's too dangerous. What if somebody finds out?"
"Nobody will find out. The kids here will talk about anything and everything, but there's one thing they won't talk about. I think you ought to look out for a fridge, Dexter. Ice-cream might not be such a bad idea after all."

* * *

Outside, Hansen and Clay were talking together near a large old tree. As soon as Hansen saw Brad and his friends, he said "I'm going to get him, John. I don't care how, but I'm going to get him. He's too confident now. I'm going to watch everything he does, and I'll have him, and that'll be the end of him at this school. No more excuses, no more next years, nothing. Finished. Basta."
"Don't let it eat you up," said Clay. "He's got to leave one day. He takes his A-levels this year."
Hansen shook his head. "That's too long to wait. And if he fails them, he'll be back again in September."

Chapter Seven

The countryside around Hartlands was really beautiful. Only one road led to the school and that came from a small town about a mile away. The road followed a clear river that wandered slowly through flat green fields. On either side where the fields stopped, trees rose up thick and green to the tops of different hills. As this one road led only to the school, few people ever used it unless they especially wanted to visit Hartlands. And so there was always an atmosphere of quiet and peace. It was an atmosphere that many teachers and pupils enjoyed. When the stress of daily life became too much, it was so nice to walk along the road next to the river and then walk up one of the paths between the silent trees. Sometimes if there was enough time, it was possible to walk to the top of one of the hills. There, on the highest point, with a clear view over the whole area, stood a ruin. Nobody really knew what it had been, but it was a place to dream and imagine, to think what it must have been like before the walls had fallen down. Had it once been a castle? Had there been soldiers here and armies? Had there been battles in the past and celebrations in the big hall later? Was the place full of adventure? Or was it just an old building or a farmhouse that had fallen down with age?

John Clay walked up to the ruin one afternoon. Spring hadn't arrived yet, but he could feel that it wasn't very far away. It was still cold outside, but the air was fresh and light. There were sounds among the trees that told him that life was coming back after a long miserable winter. And after a long miserable day at school it did him good.

When he got to the top of the hill, to the point where he could see over the school and the countryside, he was breathing heavily. He had taken off his jacket, but now that he felt the wind, he put it on again and waited for more energy to come back.

He looked at his watch. He still had enough time before he had to walk through the dormitory and check that the pupils were doing their homework. So he carried on to the old ruin. He stood on the walls and like a young boy began to imagine he, too, was the king of the castle.

But he was not alone.

Between the sounds of the birds and the wind in the trees he heard another sound. Clay turned round. In one of the rooms of the ruin, visible because the walls were only two or three feet high, stood a pupil from Hartlands. Clay, unseen, looked more carefully until he recognized the boy as Thomas Walker.

At that moment, Thomas looked up and their eyes met. Clay jumped down from the outside wall and walked across to the pupil.

"It's a nice place," said Clay. "I like the view over the valley."

Thomas smiled. "I come here a lot. It's usually very quiet and you don't see many people, especially not from school."

Clay laughed. "It's a hard climb. I suppose most of them are too lazy to come so far. But it's worth it."

The teacher and the pupil stood together silently. They were outside the normal school situation and it suddenly seemed difficult to start a conversation.

Clay broke the ice first. "I haven't seen you for a long time. You know what it's like in the dormitory, a problem here, a problem there. You go into this room and then into another, but it's always the pupils who cause problems who get the attention. You easily forget the others."

"It's all right, Mr Clay. You needn't apologize."

"Well, I should really. Time goes by so quickly. And I promised your mother I would be there if you needed me. How do you feel now in Warren House?"

Thomas shrugged. "You know how it is, Mr Clay."

Clay said nothing. He knew that Thomas was suffering in the dormitory. He knew also that there was a world of violence and power in those rooms, a secret world that was hidden from him and that disappeared as soon as he arrived. Thomas and several others were victims in this world and he, Clay, could do nothing about it.

"You're still not very happy here, Thomas."

Thomas smiled, but it was a smile without happiness.

"How's your mother?" Clay asked in a lighter, friendlier voice.

"I'm going to see her again during the holidays." Suddenly Thomas smiled warmly. "She said in her last letter I might be able to go and live with her in Switzerland."

"It's a nice country. You'll be able to learn to ski."

"There's a boarding school near where she lives. I might be able to go there."

Clay looked at him. "Do you think it'll be better than here?"

Thomas looked down at the ground. "At least I'll be able to visit her at the weekends. Here I can't visit anybody, except a few relatives I hardly know."

Clay looked at his watch. "It's getting late. We'll have to go down to the school now." Together they walked along the narrow path. It was much easier and quicker now that they were going down the hill.

* * *

"Does Brad give you any trouble?" asked Clay.

Thomas shook his head. "Not as long as I do what he wants."

"Too many people seem to do what he wants."

Thomas said nothing.

"He's the boss in Warren House, I suppose," said Clay.

"You've seen how strong he is. I have no chance against him."

"There are some people who are stronger than he is, Thomas."

"I don't know any."

They walked quickly along the narrow path until they came out on the road to Hartlands. When he saw that the school was so near, Clay said quickly, "Why does Brad have so much power in the school? What has he got over all of you. It can't be just because he's stronger than you."

They jumped down onto the road that led towards the school.

"People owe him money, they owe him favours. There are a number of reasons."

At that moment they heard a car behind. Clay turned round to see a large car coming towards them from the town. As it went past, Clay recognized Bradley in the passenger seat. Brad, too, saw Clay and Thomas. He waved, but there was no smile on his face, no friendliness in his eyes.

"What reasons?" asked Clay, his eyes on the car as it raced towards the school.

But Thomas had also seen the car – and the face in the side window. "I'm sorry, Mr Clay. I'm not an informer."

John Clay fell silent and with a serious look on his face said nothing more as they walked through the school gates. Once inside the school grounds, Thomas left him as soon as possible and ran towards Warren House, while Clay followed another path towards the main building. He had no reason to go that way, but as he walked through the large heavy doors, the secretary called him from her office.

Clay walked through the open door and found a policeman with one of the pupils from his dormitory.

"It was lucky that I saw you on the path," she said. "I tried to phone your room, but obviously you weren't there."

While she talked, Clay tried to think quickly what might have happened. An accident, a crime? Had the boy stolen something from a shop?

"I would be grateful if you would have a word with this young boy," said the policeman. "We caught him on a motorbike. He was going too fast. He said it was his, but he has no papers. As you know, it's a serious offence to ride a motorbike without tax and insurance."

"Leave it with me," said Clay.

"If he can bring his documents in to the station by the end of the week, we'll forget the whole thing."

"He'll bring them," said Clay, while his eyes never left the young pupil who sat miserably on a wooden chair next to the door.

"Can I offer you anything, a cup of tea or coffee?" asked Clay.

"No, thank you. I just wanted to bring him here and make sure somebody had a good talk to him."

"Don't worry. I'll do that."

The policeman thanked Clay, said goodbye to the secretary and left. Clay kept his eyes on young Peters and he realized how true his words had been as he had talked to Thomas near the ruins: you only have time for those pupils who cause problems.

"OK," he said. "What happened?"

Chapter Eight

There was a knock on Clay's door. Clay rubbed his eyes that had become tired after correcting too much homework. He stood up from his desk and shouted, "Come in. It's open."

The door opened and Bradley walked in. Clay remembered what Thomas had said about Brad and realized that he was indeed tall, about the same size as himself, and obviously quite strong, as he was one of old Miller's favourite athletes. Few pupils would be brave enough to stand up to him.

"Good morning, Mr Clay. You wanted to see me."

Clay *had* wanted to see him and now that the moment had come, he felt a bit nervous. Clay walked across to his sofa and sat down. He pointed to a chair. "Yes," he said. "Take a seat."

Bradley sat down opposite Clay and glanced casually around the room.

"A nice place," he said. "Better than the way Morrison had it. Did you ever meet him?"

Clay shook his head.

"A strange person. He played the piano. The louder we were in the dormitory, the louder he played the piano. Crazy." Brad smiled and waited to hear why he had been invited to see John Clay. "Would you like a cup of tea while you're here?" asked Clay. "I've just made some."

"I won't say no."

Clay stood up and walked into the kitchen. He placed the teapot, cups, milk and sugar on a tray which he then carried carefully into the living-room, where he put everything on the small table between them. "Help yourself to milk and sugar."

Clay tried to sound serious, but not too strict, as if to show Brad that this wasn't going to be a friendly talk about the weather. "Thanks," said Brad and continued to look around the room. "A nice stereo. Is it new?"

Clay nodded, drinking from his tea. "I bought it last week. I don't know whether it's good or not. I've got no idea about these things."

"It's OK," said Brad. "You should have told me you wanted one. I could have got one for you. A beautiful sound, lots of power and cheaper than you think. My brother has connections."

"It's a pity I didn't know that before," said Clay, and put his cup down. "But it's your connections that I wanted to talk about."

Bradley looked puzzled. He listened carefully as he lifted the cup to his lips.

"The police caught Peters yesterday. He was going too fast on a motorbike."

"I see," said Brad, pleased that he now knew what the subject was. He sat back, prepared to listen.

"Peters tells me he bought the bike from you. He paid you, but you never gave him the documents for it. He couldn't wait, so he rode it."

"That's his problem," said Brad. "He's crazy about bikes, but his mother won't buy him one. So he asked me to sell him one. I said no. But he wouldn't stop. Then I got this bike cheap and he insisted that he wanted it, said it was his own money and he could do what he wanted with it. I said he can have it if his mother agrees. What can I do if he rides away with it?"

"The police want to see that it is really his and that it has been taxed and insured."

"I have the documents here," said Brad and took an envelope from his pocket. He passed them over the table to Clay, who opened the envelope and looked at the different papers. "Peters is going to the police station as soon as I give these to him. I hope you're satisfied. As you can see, the bike is properly taxed and insured."

Clay turned the documents over, then put them down on the table. "You seem to be quite a good businessman. Especially when you have to produce documents at the last minute."

"If you're talking about the pub, I didn't produce them at the last minute. Those documents were done properly. By me. You know, everybody wants something, but few people are prepared to work for it. Everybody in the school wanted the pub, but nobody was prepared to run it. So I took it over, and look at the thanks I get. I order drinks and sell them to the pupils. Is that a crime?"

"No, I suppose not."

"Peters wants a motorbike. His mother won't let him have one, so he buys one from me. Is that a crime?"

Clay sighed and stood up. "I suppose it isn't. But Peters could have had an accident. He could have killed somebody, or even himself."

"He didn't. But if it'll make you feel happier, I'll buy the bike back from him. He can have the money back. Then nobody has any problems."

Clay said nothing. Brad seemed to have an answer to everything. He walked over to the window and looked out at the quiet grounds. "Does Thomas still come and visit you?"

The question hit Clay like an unexpected blow. He turned round and their eyes suddenly met.

"Why?" he asked quietly.

"He's not very popular in school. He needs a friend, I guess."

"Is that a crime?"

Brad smiled. "No, it isn't. But I suppose if I was looking for an informer, he'd be the perfect person – how should I say? – to cultivate. He's shy, isolated, he has few friends, but he's on the inside. He knows what's happening."

"Get out," said Clay.

Brad stood up. "Goodbye, Mr Clay," he said politely. "And thanks for the tea."

* * *

The group of boys surrounded Thomas when he was alone on one of the school fields. He had just finished a game of tennis with another pupil and was returning to his room when they walked towards him and suddenly made a circle with Thomas in the middle.

Thomas knew the faces well – Brad, Dexter, Steve, Mitch, all Brad's friends, all older boys.

"What do you want?" he asked, feeling that they would never let him pass.

Brad was holding a rugby ball. He threw it lightly in the air and caught it again.

"I thought we'd play a game of rugby, Thomas. How would you like to join us?"

"I can't play rugby."

"Everybody can play rugby. It's the main sport in this school."

"I don't like it."

"That's a different thing. Is it too rough for you?"

The other boys grinned.

"Does our little boy not want to get dirty? What will mummy say if his trousers and shirt are dirty?"

The circle of boys was laughing openly. Thomas felt nervous and frightened. He knew that his face was red. His legs were beginning to tremble.

"I don't want to play," he said. "Can I get past, please? I'd like to go to my room."

"We've decided you're going to play with us," said Brad. Brad threw the ball, quickly and very hard. "Here, catch."

Thomas moved his arms to stop the ball, but it hit him before he could catch it and it fell to the floor. Dexter moved forward and picked it up. Thomas was still trapped in the middle of the circle.

"That wasn't very good," said Brad. "Try again."

This time Dexter threw the ball, again hard and very fast. He aimed at Thomas's head. Thomas lifted his arms to cover his face, and the ball hit his shoulder. Another pupil picked up the ball quickly.

"I noticed you were with Clay the other day. Did you go for a walk with him?"

"What's wrong with that?" asked Thomas nervously.

"What did you tell him?"

"How do you mean?"

"Here, catch the ball," said Dexter and Thomas had to turn quickly to see who was throwing it. This time Thomas caught it, and the pupils jumped on him.

For anybody who was walking along one of the paths, the scene would have seemed harmless: a group of boys were practising rugby. They were rolling around on the grass and laughing. Nobody would have thought it was serious. But underneath the five boys Thomas was trying to shout for help. Nobody could hear him because somebody had a hand over his mouth. The others were punching and hitting him. When they stood up, Thomas lay hurt and dirty on the grass. Brad picked up the ball as if the game was over. He laughed as if it had all been good fun. He threw the ball lightly to Dexter, who threw it to another friend. They waited until Thomas sat up.

He was hurt. His body ached where they had punched him in the face and stomach, in the neck and on the back. But why? What had he done now? Or had he done nothing at all? They just felt like it, they did it out of boredom.

"If you know what's good for you," said Brad, "you'll keep your mouth shut when you're with Clay. Do you hear me?"

Thomas nodded and the boys walked away. They went slowly across the field towards the gym, so that everything seemed to be really harmless.

Thomas walked back to his room. He hoped that he wouldn't see anybody, and he was lucky. Few people were on the paths, and nobody was in the building as he pushed the heavy doors open. He was in pain as he climbed the stairs to the Upper Dormitory, where his room was. He went down the dark lightless corridor to his door, but just then John Clay came out of his flat and walked towards him.

Clay stopped when he saw the younger pupil.

"What happened to you?" he asked.

"I've just had a game of rugby," said Thomas. "With some of the others."

He tried to unlock his door as quickly as possible and get into his room so that he didn't have to talk about it.

"You usually wear a rugby shirt and shorts when you play. You're wearing your tennis shirt and it's dirty."

Thomas kept his face away from Clay so that the teacher couldn't see anything. But Clay had already seen more than enough. "You're hurt," he said. "Who did it? Was it Brad?"

Thomas said nothing. Nervously he tried to unlock the door, and the more he pushed the key, the more difficult it seemed to open the door. Clay put a hand on the boy's shoulder. "Give me the key. I'll open it."

Thomas let his hand go from the key and Clay unlocked the door. When he looked into Thomas's face he could see that the boy was fighting hard to stop the tears, that he couldn't hold them back much longer.

"Go into your room and take those clothes off," he said softly. "Have a hot shower, and if you want to talk to me, come to my rooms later. I'll be there. But you don't have to say anything if you don't want. I'll make you a hot drink and you can stay with me until you feel better."

Thomas nodded and went into his room, his head low, tears on the edge of his eyes, and shut the door behind him.

Clay stood in the corridor for a few moments and felt the anger inside him, anger because he felt so helpless. Only a few feet away, on the other side of a wooden door was somebody in pain, but he, Clay, might as well be on the other side of the world.

* * *

An hour later there was a knock on Clay's door. Clay got up immediately and went to the door. When he opened it, Thomas was there.

"Come in," said Clay and the boy walked quietly into the living-room.

He had had a shower and was wearing clean clothes, but Clay could see clearly where the boys had hit him.

"You said there were people in Hartlands who were stronger than Brad."

Clay nodded, his face serious. "That's right, Thomas."

"Could you stop him, Mr Clay?"

Clay sat down slowly and asked Thomas to sit down on the sofa.

"I can stop him, Thomas."

"Can you make sure that he won't do anything to me again?"

Clay nodded. "I can do that, Thomas. I promise you he won't do anything to anybody again. I promise you that."

Thomas sat down and looked down at his hands.

"I've got something to tell you, Mr Clay."

Chapter Nine

Hansen listened carefully to what John Clay told him.

"I don't believe it," he said. "I just don't believe it."

He sat down and ran his fingers through his hair. "Thomas told you this? Where did he get his information? I mean, this is unbelievable. It's what I've always been waiting for."

John Clay was standing in the middle of the room, his hands in his pockets. He had come straight to Hansen's rooms after his conversation with Thomas and he had been in such a hurry that he hadn't even taken off his jacket.

"Have you told the head?" asked Hansen.

Clay shook his head. "I went to his office, but I wasn't allowed to speak to him. The secretary said he was in a meeting with the school's trustees and didn't want to see anybody."

"That's right," said Hansen. "I forgot. He'll be with them all day. What time is it?"

"Four o'clock."

"And what time did Thomas say? Eight?"

Clay nodded.

"We'll just have to wait."

"What do you think Mr Graham will say if we do this without him?"

"What can he say?" said Hansen. "This is the biggest thing we've ever had here. I need a coffee. Will you drink a cup with me?"

Clay nodded and took off his jacket. "I've got some time until I have to check the dormitory. What's the meeting with the school governors about?"

"No idea," said Hansen. "Probably money. That's usually the only reason they ever come here. We're probably spending too much and earning too little. That's the problem with a private school. Just like Brad and his pub, we have expenses and there are bills to pay. And Mr Graham has to find the money to pay them."

"Make Brad the headmaster," said Clay.

"That is not a bad idea," said Hansen from the kitchen. "But if he ran this place the way he ran the pub, he would make a nice profit and we would earn nothing. Sugar and milk?"

"Both," said Clay.

* * *

The meeting with the school's trustees was indeed about money. In the headmaster's office the small group of men and women sat at a round table, documents and papers in front of them. On the documents were figures: numbers and calculations.

The chairman took a drink from a glass of water and, taking off his glasses, looked seriously at his colleagues. "That is the financial situation," he said, and lifted the papers on the table in front of him. "We are losing pupils, and so we are losing money. We can't afford to do either."

Nobody said anything. Facts were facts, and the figures spoke for themselves.

"The question is, why are we losing pupils? I have here some letters from worried parents. Perhaps you would like to see them, Mr Graham?"

"I receive them, too. I know their contents. Too much freedom, too little discipline."

"But these parents pay for this school. These parents pay for your teachers, Mr Graham. Three pupils go and one teacher must go."

"That is putting it a little too simply," said Mr Graham. "The majority of parents are happy with the way this school is run. There are a few parents who still do not understand what we are doing here. It takes time to introduce a new programme, and we need time."

"If we had a waiting list of parents who wanted to send their children here, then I would say, yes, you can have all the time you need. But unfortunately, that is not the case. At the moment we still have too few pupils to meet the costs of the school. We cannot afford to experiment, Mr Graham. We have to make sure that those parents who send their children do not take them away again."

"When you offered me the job, you knew what I wanted to do here. I made no secret of my plans and ideas."

"We still believe that your ideas are good for Hartlands; we still believe that you will make this a school where pupils feel happy and parents will know that their children are in good hands. But the economic situation has changed dramatically. We do not have a long list of parents who want to send their children here."

"Not yet."

"But we are worried about the present financial situation of the school," said one of the trustees very quietly. "And if parents complain now, then we must listen to what they say carefully and see how we can help them."

"You mean we must persuade them to leave their children here?" Mr Graham looked at the trustees seriously. "We need an open and friendly atmosphere here. This school is not a machine that forces pupils to learn; we don't sit on them until they have done their homework. There are lots of other schools in the country that offer that. We teach them to help each other, because those are the qualities they will need when they leave."

Mr Graham stopped to look out of the window as if a sudden thought had come to him.

"And even if we introduce stricter methods, as some parents want, it will not – if I have understood you properly – improve our financial situation."

"That is our main point, Mr Graham," said the chairman. "We are not saying we must return to stricter methods, but we cannot lose more pupils. You were correct with what you said before. We must meet those parents who are unhappy and make sure that their children stay here. Our experts have studied the figures and the costs from all sides and would like to suggest the following plan."

Mr Graham sat back, interested, while the chairman put on his glasses again and began to read from a document that the headmaster did not have.

"We suggest that we keep the numbers of pupils as we have them now and reduce the number of people who are employed here."

Mr Graham was shocked. "Could you repeat that, please?" he said, as if it was possible that he had heard something completely different.

The chairman looked again at his paper. "Our experts have calculated that if we reduce the number of people who are employed here and keep the present number of pupils, we will cover our costs. And only if we do this."

"And can you suggest how we reduce that number?" said Mr Graham angrily.

"We feel that should be your decision, Mr Graham. You know your colleagues best. But we would suggest two teachers, two people from the kitchen and one from the gardening staff. Obviously you will want to keep those teachers who are good, but it might be easier to adopt the American principle: last hired, first fired."

Mr Graham looked down at the papers on his table, people, jobs, ideas, plans, dreams – all reduced to numbers, all seen in the form of profit or loss.

"I will have to look at the separate contracts before I make any decisions." He breathed in deeply and pushed his chair back from the table.

"May I suggest that we have a break?"

Chapter Ten

It was evening in Hartlands and already dark. John Clay and Peter Hansen were sitting on a wooden bench in a quiet corner of the school grounds. It was a favourite place for those pupils or teachers who wanted to sit somewhere quietly where they could read, talk or simply enjoy the surroundings. But for Hansen and Clay the gardens had another advantage. From here they could see the rooms of Warren House and they could see quite clearly whose lights were on and whose were off.

"This is such a nice place," said Hansen. "One of the nicest places I've ever seen. You know we should all be really happy here. And what's the situation?" He sat back, his arms along the top of the bench and looked up into the dark night. "Look at that sky, the stars; the air is so fresh. How many people can enjoy this?"

"Which is Dexter's room?" asked Clay, not listening to what Hansen was saying.

"Lower Dormitory," said Hansen, his thoughts brought suddenly back to reality and why they were sitting there. "The third from the left. The light is on."

Clay looked across at the dark building, where only a few lights were burning.

"So they're already in there?"

Hansen nodded. "We should wait a little longer, though, until the film club has started."

"What is the film tonight?"

"A western, as far as I know."

Clay looked down at his hands. "I only hope Thomas is right."

"We'll soon see."

The two men sat in silence. Neither of them spoke as they waited and watched and saw more lights go out, until only the one light was on in the Lower Dormitory.

"It doesn't look like Dexter is going to the film club tonight," said Hansen. He looked at his watch. "Perhaps we should give them five more minutes, let them feel a little safer, then pay them a visit."

"I notice the head has called a special teachers' meeting for tomorrow morning. Any idea what it's about?"

Hansen shook his head. "All I know is that we will discuss something that the head hasn't planned to discuss, namely Brad. If we catch him tonight, then tomorrow I'll drop the whole thing onto the table."

"Do you think he'll be able to talk his way out?"

"Who? Graham or Brad?"

"Both."

"Impossible. The head will have to throw Brad out now. There is no way he can keep him in this school now. – Not this time. And we'll have proof."

"I need to be sure," said Clay.

"You can be sure. As sure as I'm sitting here."

Clay was beginning to feel nervous and impatient. He wanted to get up and go to the room now, but he knew they had to wait a little longer.

"I see the light is still on in the head's office. His meeting with the trustees is surely over."

"It finished at six, but he didn't come to evening meal."

"I wonder what he's doing in there," said Clay. "He's in that office most evenings till late."

"He's probably working on his plans and dreams for a new and better school."

"Do you think he'll ever succeed?"

"I'm sure he will. I hope he will. I just wonder whether we will be there to see that new school. And I certainly hope he doesn't have people like Brad to ruin it. But how do you combine ideas and business? Tell me that, John." Hansen paused and looked at his watch. "It's quarter to eight."

Clay stood up slowly. "OK. Let's get it over with."

The two men walked slowly along the dark path to Warren House. The only sounds they could hear were their feet on the dry stones, and from the film club the gunfire and music of a western.

They pushed the large heavy doors of Warren House open and stepped into the warm building. Outside, the night air had become cold. The whole building seemed to be empty; they could feel its silence in their ears. Old buildings have a different atmosphere when people have left them. They are like grandparents who can sit down and rest after the screaming children have gone home. The dormitory was resting quietly now. A clock ticked, but that was all they could hear.

At the top of the stairs they looked down the long corridor. Only a few of the lights were on, so it was dark along the walls and between the cupboards. Nobody was moving; there were no voices in any of the rooms, except in Dexter's.

Hansen and Clay walked quietly down the dark corridor and stopped in front of Dexter's door. Inside the room they could hear music, the voices of boys and girls, glasses and bottles and a chair as somebody moved.

"A nice little party," said Hansen. "They've probably got two or three girls from the town. It's a pity to stop it."

He tapped gently against the door. The voices stopped at once. The two men could feel controlled silence on the other side of the door, as eyes looked at each other and they tried to guess who was outside.

"Who is it?" came a voice.

"Open the door," said Hansen strictly, and banged heavily against it. "Open it or I'll break it open."

* * *

Inside the room there was panic.

"Cigarettes out of the window," commanded Brad quickly.

"Hide the bottles, put them under the bed, in a cupboard, anywhere."

Pupils started to move quickly, they hid bottles, they threw cigarettes out of the open window.

"What do we do with Jackie?" one of the boys asked. Brad looked at the teenage girl. She had definitely drunk too much. She had her arms round her boyfriend's shoulders. Her eyes were closed as she listened to the music. She hadn't noticed what was happening.

"Hide her," said Brad quickly. "Come on, hurry up. Push her under the bed."

Before her boyfriend could say anything, other pupils pulled the girl from him and pushed her under the bed like an old sack. Jackie's eyes shot open, but Brad whispered in her ear. "Don't say a word. Do you hear?" Jackie nodded and closed her eyes again.

Brad stood up and quickly looked round the room. Outside, Hansen was still banging heavily against the door and it sounded as if he meant to break it open.

"Frank, open the door," said Brad. "Dexter, quickly, a bottle of aftershave."

"Wha.." Dexter began to say, but Brad never let him finish.

"A bottle of aftershave. Quickly."

Dexter took a bottle and threw it across the room to Brad, who caught it and threw it on the floor. It broke at once and the smell filled the room.

At that moment Frank opened the door and the two teachers marched in.

Hansen spoke first. He smelled the aftershave and saw the broken bottle on the floor. "What's the idea of that?"

"Frank tried to open the door so quickly that he hit a table and the bottle fell off."

"That's a good story. I'm sure that's what happened."

"Are you looking for somebody?" asked Dexter politely.

"Most of the pupils are at the film club. I'm sure that's more interesting than our party."

"That's where you're wrong," said Hansen. "Perhaps your party is more interesting than you think."

He looked at the different faces. Some he knew, some he didn't. Some were obviously boys and girls from the town. Nobody said anything as he looked around the room, let his eyes run along the shelves, over the table, the bed. Carefully he opened a drawer in one of the cupboards and with one hand felt what was inside.

"Hey," said Dexter. "Those are my private things. You can't do that. You've got no right ..."

Hansen interrupted him. "I've got no right? Tell me what I've got no right to do."

"You've got no right to do that. Mr Graham says our rooms are private. You can't just open drawers and cupboards without a reason."

"Perhaps I've got a reason," said Hansen. "A very good reason."

Dexter's face went pale and several of the others began to feel worried and nervous. But then Brad stood up and smiled warmly.

"All right," he said with a friendly voice. "Let's stop the arguments. There's no reason to get angry or excited."

He walked into the middle of the room, until he stood between Dexter and the two teachers. "Let's admit we're wrong. We've broken the school rules. We've invited some boys and girls from the town without permission. We're now having a party and we've got alcohol in the rooms. There's no reason to get aggressive because we've been caught."

Very coolly and calmly he threw back the blankets on the bed and took out the bottles that had been hidden there. "They've caught us. Let the teachers have some fun, too."

"Why don't you shut up!" said Hansen.

Brad held out the bottles as if he had heard nothing. "Here you are, Mr Hansen. We're sorry."

"We're not looking for alcohol," said Clay suddenly. "And we're not looking for visitors from the town."

"What do you want then?" said Brad harmlessly. "A cup of coffee?"

"What's that?" asked Hansen. He had suddenly seen something large and white in a corner.

"A fridge," said Dexter in a perfectly normal voice.

"A fridge?" asked Hansen angrily. "Why do you need a fridge here?"

"We sell ice-cream in the summer. We've always done it."

"Does Mr Graham know about this?"

"We only bought it a couple of days ago," said Brad. "If Mr Graham insists, I'm sure Dexter will take it out."

"There's nothing in the school rules that says we can't have a fridge," said Dexter.

Hansen walked towards the fridge. It was the kind you found in shops with the lid on top, so you had to put your arms in to get the ice-cream.

"OK," he said. "If you sell ice-cream, then we'll have one. I feel like an ice-cream. What do you say John?"

"We're not selling at the moment," said Dexter. "We're closed."

"Well, open. Get me an ice-cream," said Hansen. "Now."

Again Brad took control. He went to the fridge and opened the lid. "What would you like?" he asked patiently.

"Vanilla," said Hansen. "And chocolate for Mr Clay."

Brad lifted the lid and put his hand into the open fridge. At that moment, in the quiet room, they all heard a girl sneeze.

"Quiet!" shouted Hansen. "Everybody."

Nobody moved or spoke. Then Hansen saw Jackie's feet under the bed. "John, she's under the bed," he shouted.

Immediately Clay jumped across the room and grabbed the girl's feet. He pulled her out as far as he could.

"I'm sorry," she shouted. "Dust got in my nose. I couldn't help it."

At that moment, while Hansen and Clay were busy with the girl, Brad took a plastic bag from the fridge and threw it across the room to Dexter, who caught it like a ball and ran straight towards the door.

Hansen saw the bag fly through the air and shouted, "Dexter, stay where you are."

Both men dropped the girl and tried to catch Dexter as he pulled the door open, but there was chaos in the room as all the pupils jumped to their feet.

"John, he's got something. Stop him quickly."

But neither men could get near him as the pupils filled the door, the one trying to get out of the room faster than the next.

Hansen pulled the girl to her feet.

"Get your hands off me!" she screamed. "I haven't done anything. I said, leave me alone."

Hansen ignored her. "John," he shouted, "where's Dexter? He took something out of the fridge. We've got to get him."

But Clay was helpless. "There are too many people in the door," he shouted back. "I can't get out."

Jackie fought and struggled, but Hansen held her tightly. He turned to Brad who hadn't moved. "OK," he said. "Where is it?"

"You're too late," said Brad.

"I want the police here," said Hansen angrily. "I'm going to pull this place to pieces."

"You won't find anything," said Brad. "It's probably in the woods. You'll have to dig up the whole forest to find anything."

Hansen turned away. He felt the hate and frustration in his stomach. "OK," he said. "We take the girl to hospital."

Jackie kicked and pulled. "Leave me alone," she screamed. "I've already told you. I haven't done anything."

"That won't prove anything," said Brad confidently. "She has only drunk some alcohol. If she had taken anything, it wouldn't mean a thing. She's from the town. She has lots of friends there."

Hansen, furious that the situation had gone this way, turned to Clay. "Where's Dexter?" he said.

"He's gone," said Clay. "I've only got two arms. There was no way I could catch him."

"I think we should all go to Mr Graham."

Hansen took the girl and walked towards the door, but John Clay didn't follow him. Clay stood opposite Brad, face to face. Hansen stopped.

"John ...," he said.

Then he saw Clay's right hand suddenly make a fist.

"John, ... No!" shouted Hansen. "Don't! That's what he wants."

But Hansen was too late. Clay's right hand shot towards Brad's head.

"John!" Hansen shouted and forgot Jackie as he tried to stop Clay.

Jackie, freed, ran towards the open door and out of the room.

Chapter Eleven

The meeting with Mr Graham the following morning started at 9 o'clock, so the first lesson was free for all the pupils. That meant that after breakfast they could do some homework, play games or simply go back to bed for an hour while the teachers sat silently and seriously round a large table in the school library. Some pupils looked curiously through the windows to see what was so important that the teachers had to come together so early. Some even hoped to hear a sentence or two through the closed doors so they could be the first to tell the news to the others. Most of them had already heard what had happened in the dormitory the evening before, and the wildest stories were already going from room to room, but few could have imagined what the meeting was really about.

"As you know," Mr Graham said to the teachers around him. "I had a long meeting with the school's trustees yesterday. Unfortunately, our financial situation is more serious than we thought and it is the subject which I would like to discuss with you this morning."

Hansen interrupted immediately. "I don't want to be impolite, Mr Graham," he said. "But yesterday evening when we were in your office, you said that we would discuss the Bradley case first." Hansen turned to the other teachers. His eyes were going from face to face as he talked to them. "You have probably already heard that Mr Clay and myself went into John Dexter's room. We had information that Brad had started to deal in drugs and was actually selling them that evening. While Mr Clay and I were in the room, Bradley took a plastic bag out of a fridge that was in the room and threw it to Dexter. Dexter ran out of the room with it. We believe there were drugs in that bag. They also had alcohol in the room. There were some boys and girls from the town, and one girl was drunk. It is, I feel, our duty now to decide what we are going to do with Bradley and his friends."

Hansen sat back, confident. Several teachers nodded. Like the pupils, they had heard of the scene in Dexter's room. But the headmaster lifted a hand to tell everybody that they should please be quiet while he gave his answer.

"Mr Hansen," he said quietly. "After our conversation yesterday evening, I talked with Bradley. In fact, he was in my office till after midnight. I even called his parents and discussed the situation with them on the phone. It is true that drugs are coming into this school. Bradley has admitted that drugs were hidden in his room, but denies that he had at any time sold any drugs. He also denies that he ever intended to sell any drugs. He knows that what he had done was against the law. However, he also told me how drugs have been entering this school and the names of the people in the area are who are supplying our young people. I intend to give this information to the police later today." Hansen threw his pencil on the table and sat forward angrily. Other teachers protested.

"Surely you don't believe what that boy says?" said Hansen.

"If we throw him out now, we are not solving any problems. Or do you believe that drugs will no longer come into this school if I expel Bradley? It is our job now to get proper control of the situation and make sure that drugs no longer find their way into this school." Hansen began to protest loudly, but the headmaster continued. "There are also a number of difficulties to the situation which I needn't stress. Mr Clay hit Bradley in front of the other pupils. That does not help our case; it only makes it worse. You did not even find anything. You only saw a plastic bag. This could create a scandal if the story became known publicly. It would ruin the image and the reputation of this school."

"To keep him is a scandal," said Hansen dryly. "And Dexter would never have run out of that room if there had only been ice-cream in that bag."

"We don't know what was in that bag, Mr Hansen. As I said, I have talked with Bradley's father. Bradley is leaving at the end of the school year as soon as he has completed his A-levels. And if he fails, you can be certain that I will not accept him back." "Why not now? Why not today?" said Hansen impatiently.

"At the end of the school year, Mr Hansen," the headmaster repeated.

"I needn't stress how generous the Bradleys have been to this school in the past." The person who had spoken was Mr Richards, the deputy headmaster.

"What Bradley did was a serious crime," said Hansen. "Hand him over to the police. He belongs in prison. That's the only place where he will realize how many mistakes he has made."

"I needn't remind you, Mr Hansen," said the headmaster, "that you had information, but you have no proof. We only have Bradley's own words. He confessed and told us what he knew – if he could have one last chance."

"In other words he has done a deal with you. We are covering up," said Hansen. "We are letting him walk away free."

"If we can find any proof of Bradley's activities, Mr Hansen, concrete proof, then I will take that boy to the police. And he knows it. Until he leaves, and even after he has left, he must live with the fear that he is only free until we find something."

Mr Graham looked at his watch as if to say they had spent enough time on that topic.

"As I mentioned at the beginning of our meeting, the trustees and the banks are worried about the financial situation of our school. At the moment we are spending more money than we are earning, and that is leading to a large deficit. I must reduce the deficit by the end of the school year. We have examined all the possibilities and, unfortunately, I must inform you that I can no longer employ the full number of teachers we have at Hartlands.

I'm sorry that I have to say this, but I have no other choice."

Nobody had expected this. Faces went white as several teachers suddenly realized that their jobs were in danger. In that short pause they thought of their families, their homes, their ages – all except Hansen who played angrily with a piece of paper. John Clay wasn't even listening. He was looking sadly out of the library window, thinking of the promise he had made, a promise he had not kept.

"I have done my best," said Mr Graham, "to be fair and keep as many employees as I can. But after all my calculations I must tell you that I have to dismiss two teachers and four members of staff from the gardens and kitchens. With regard to the teachers I have chosen those who have been with us the shortest time."

Nervously Mr Graham took two envelopes and stood up.

"Mr Hansen," he said quietly.

Hansen froze. His eyes widened. The colour left his face until it was grey with shock. Slowly he turned his head to look at the headmaster.

"I'm sorry," said Mr Graham.

Hansen took the envelope and looked at it as if he couldn't believe what was happening.

"And Mr Clay," the headmaster went on.

John Clay looked away from the window and saw the headmaster with an envelope in his hand.

"Thank you," said Clay and put it on the table next to his books for the next lesson.

Mr Graham went back to his chair at the head of the table.

"There was no other way," he said, as if he was trying to apologize for something he didn't agree with. "If we do nothing, then we will have to shut this school one year from now. The banks gave me no other choice. I have called a separate meeting for the kitchen and garden staff for 10 o'clock. I am sorry that we have come to such an unfortunate situation."

Chapter Twelve

Later that day Thomas Walker went to his room. The last lesson was over and he had some time before he had to be at his desk and do his homework. He unlocked his door and went in. He sat down on his bed and started to repair his broken cassette-recorder. A cassette was trapped and the tape was blocking the heads.

Time passed, and he slowly forgot the world of Hartlands as he carefully pulled the tape out of the small recorder, until suddenly there was a knock on his door.

Thomas looked up. There was another knock, not urgent or violent, so he got up and went to the door. When he opened it, his heart sank and he felt himself tremble with fear. Brad was standing there. He was smiling when he said, "Hallo, Thomas. How are you?"

Thomas's knees began to shake and his throat felt dry.

"What do you want?" he asked.

Brad smiled. "You," he said and pushed Thomas back into the room.

Vocabulary

adv. = adverb, *pl.* = plural, *sb.* = somebody, *sth.* = something

A **academic** [ækə'demɪk] (geistes)wissenschaftlich
accountant [ə'kaʊntənt] Buchhalter/in
accounts *(pl.)* [ə'kaʊnts] Geschäftsbücher
(to) **admit** [əd'mɪt] zugeben
(to) **adopt** [ə'dɒpt] übernehmen, zu eigen machen
all the same trotzdem
(to) **allow** [ə'laʊ] erlauben, gestatten, zulassen
along: **I'll be along in a minute.** Ich bin in einer Minute da.
anger ['æŋgə] Ärger, Zorn, Wut
announcement [ə'naʊnsmənt] Ankündigung
as soon as sobald als
as though als ob
audience ['ɔːdjəns] Publikum
authority [ɔː'θɒrətɪ] Autorität
awake: (to) **be awake** [ə'weɪk] wach sein

B **back**: **Is he back to his old tricks?** Macht er wieder seine alten Dummheiten/Streiche?
(to) **back out** sich zurückziehen
(to) **bang** [bæŋ] (zu)knallen
bar [bɑː] Theke
basically *(adv.)* ['beɪsɪkəlɪ] grundlegend
(to) **be no good** nichts taugen
(to) **be to do sth.** etwas tun sollen
beer [bɪə] Bier
bench [bentʃ] Bank

(to) **bend** [bend] beugen
bent → (to) **bend**
bike *hier:* = **motorbike**
(to) **block** [blɒk] blockieren
blow [bləʊ] Luftzug, Brise
(to) **boo** [buː] buhen
(to) **break up** zerstören
breathless [ˈbreθlɪs] außer Atem, atemlos
briefcase [ˈbriːfkeɪs] Aktentasche
(to) **burst** [bɜːst] zerspringen
by now mittlerweile, schon

C (to) **calculate** [ˈkælkjʊleɪt] errechnen, kalkulieren
calculation [kælkjʊˈleɪʃn] Kalkulation, Berechnung
can: I can't help it. Ich kann nichts dafür.
cancer [ˈkænsə] Krebs
career [kəˈrɪə] Karriere, Laufbahn
case Koffer; Aktentasche
casually [ˈkæʒʊəlɪ] gleichgültig, beiläufig
cell [sel] (Gefängnis-)Zelle
chairman [ˈtʃeəmən] Vorsitzender
charming [ˈtʃɑːmɪŋ] charmant
chest [tʃest] Brust(kasten)
(to) **claim** [kleɪm] zurückfordern; behaupten
claw [klɔː] Klaue, Kralle
coffin [ˈkɒfɪn] Sarg
colleague [ˈkɒliːg] Kollege, Kollegin
(to) **combine** [kɒmˈbaɪn] verbinden
command [kəˈmɑːnd] Befehl
comment [ˈkɒment] Bemerkung, Kommentar
committee [kəˈmɪtɪ] Komitee, Ausschuß
concrete [ˈkɒŋkriːt] konkret
(to) **confess** [kənˈfes] zugeben, (Schuld) bekennen
contents [ˈkɒntents] Inhalt

contract ['kɒntrækt] Vertrag
(to) **cover up for sb.** jn. decken
crate [kreɪt] Kasten
cripple ['krɪpl] Krüppel
(to) **crowd** sich drängen
cultivate ['kʌltɪveɪt] pflegen, sich warmhalten
cynical ['sɪnɪkl] zynisch

D **deal** [di:l] Geschäft, Handel
(to) **deal (in)** handeln (mit)
(to) **decorate** ['dekəreɪt] dekorieren; tapezieren
(to) **deliver** [dɪ'lɪvə] liefern
(to) **deny** [dɪ'naɪ] ab-, bestreiten
deposit [dɪ'pɒzɪt] Pfand
deputy ['depjʊtɪ] stellvertretend
determined [dɪ'tɜ:mɪnd] (fest) entschlossen
(to) **dig up** [dɪg] umgraben
(to) **disappear** [dɪsə'pɪə] verschwinden
(to) **dismiss** [dɪs'mɪs] entlassen
(to) **do without sth.** ohne etwas auskommen
doorman Türsteher
doorway Türöffnung
dormitory ['dɔ:mətrɪ] Etage mit Schlafräumen
drama ['drɑ:mə] Schauspiel; Dramatik
dramatically [drə'mætɪkəlɪ] dramatisch
drawer ['drɔ:ə] Schublade
drug [drʌg] Droge
duty ['dju:tɪ] Pflicht

E (to) **eat: don't let it eat you up** laß dich nicht davon fertigmachen
(to) **echo** ['ekəʊ] widerhallen
education Erziehung

either jede(r, s); beides
embarrassed [ɪm'bærəst] verlegen, peinlich berührt
(to) **envy** ['envɪ] jn. (um etwas) beneiden
equally *(adv.)* ['iːkwəlɪ] ebenso, gleich(ermaßen)
escape: his name escaped him sein Name ist/war ihm entfallen
(to) **examine** [ɪg'zæmɪn] untersuchen, prüfen
excitement [ɪk'saɪtmənt] Aufregung
(to) **expel** [ɪk'spel] verweisen, hinauswerfen
expense [ɪk'spens] Unkosten
(to) **explode** [ɪk'spləʊd] ausbrechen; explodieren

F

farce [fɑːs] Farce, „Theater"
favourite Favorit/in
fear [fɪə] Furcht, Angst
(to) **feel like sth.** auf etwas Lust haben
figure Zahl, Ziffer
fist [fɪst] Faust
(to) **flush** [flʌʃ] spülen
forward ['fɔːwəd] nach vorne
(to) **frighten** ['fraɪtn] erschrecken, Angst bekommen
frightened ['fraɪtnd] verängstigt, erschreckt
frightening ['fraɪtnɪŋ] erschreckend
frustrated [frʌ'streɪtɪd] frustriert, entmutigt
furious ['fjʊərɪəs] wütend

G

gently ['dʒentlɪ] sanft
(to) **get drunk** sich betrinken
(to) **get physical** handgreiflich werden
(to) **get sth. over with** etwas hinter sich bringen
(to) **get used to** sich gewöhnen an
(to) **glance** [glɑːns] einen Blick werfen, flüchtig blicken
(to) **go** *hier:* (hin)kommen

(to) **go on: What's going on?** Was ist los?
(to) **go over sth.** durchgehen, durchsprechen
governors *(pl.)* [ˈgʌvənəz] Vorstand, Direktorium
(to) **grab** [græb] ergreifen, packen
grateful [ˈgreɪtfʊl] dankbar
(to) **grin** [grɪn] grinsen
ground Gelände
gunfire [ˈgʌnfaɪə] Schießerei

H (to) **have a good talk to sb.** mit jm. ein ernstes Wort reden
(to) **have a word with sb.** mit jm. ein ernstes Wort reden
head = headmaster
head Tonkopf
heartbeat [ˈhɑːtbiːt] Herzschlag
hell [hel] Hölle
(to) **hurry** eilen, hasten

I **idea: What's the idea of that?** Was soll das?
immediately [ɪˈmiːdjətlɪ] unmittelbar, sofort, direkt
(to) **impress** [ɪmˈpres] beeindrucken, imponieren
impressive [ɪmˈpresɪv] eindrucksvoll, imposant
in time rechtzeitig
indeed [ɪnˈdiːd] tatsächlich
informer [ɪnˈfɔːmə] Informant/in, Spitzel
inquiry [ɪnˈkwaɪərɪ] Untersuchung
(to) **insist** [ɪnˈsɪst] bestehen (auf)
insurance [ɪnˈʃɔːrəns] Versicherung
insure [ɪnˈʃɔː] versichern
(to) **intend** [ɪnˈtend] vorhaben, beabsichtigen
intention [ɪnˈtenʃn] Absicht
(to) **interrupt** [ɪntəˈrʌpt] unterbrechen

J **judge** [dʒʌdʒ] Richter/in
jury [ˈdʒʊərɪ] (die) Geschworenen, Jury

K (to) **keep an eye on sth./sb.** etwas/jn. im Auge behalten
(to) **kick (in)** [kɪk] (ein)treten

L **late night film** Spätfilm
(to) **lay a finger on sb**. [leɪ] jm. etwas nachweisen; jn. zu fassen kriegen
(to) **lean (against)** [liːn] lehnen (gegen)
(to) **leave sth. to sb.** etwas jm. überlassen
lid [lɪd] Deckel
lightless unbeleuchtet
limit [ˈlɪmɪt] Grenze
lock [lɒk] Schloß
(to) **look into** untersuchen, prüfen
loss [lɒs] Verlust
lot Menge, Haufen, Bande
lower [ləʊə] unter
luck: bad luck [lʌk] Pech
luggage [ˈlʌgɪdʒ] Gepäck

M (to) **make up one's mind** sich eine Meinung bilden, sich entscheiden
mass [mæs] Masse
mattress [ˈmætrɪs] Matratze
(to) **mean to do sth.** etwas tun wollen
(to) **mean: Does it mean anything to you?** Sagt dir das irgendwas?
(to) **meet the costs** die Kosten decken

N **namely** *(adv.)* [ˈneɪmlɪ] nämlich
neat [niːt] ordentlich, adrett
(to) **need** müssen; brauchen
no-man's land [ˈnəʊmænz lænd] Niemandsland
non-profit (making) [ˈprɒfɪt] gemeinnützig
nonsense [ˈnɒnsəns] Nonsens, Unsinn
not really nicht ganz
now and again von Zeit zu Zeit, gelegentlich

O (to) **obey** [əˈbeɪ] gehorchen
offence [əˈfens] Vergehen, Verstoß
on the inside eingeweiht sein
once sobald
one by one einer nach dem anderen
opportunity [ɒpəˈtjuːnətɪ] (günstige) Gelegenheit
order [ˈɔːdə] Anweisung
other: the other day neulich
(to) **owe** [əʊ] schulden

P **pale** [peɪl] blaß
(to) **pause** [pɔːz] innehalten
(to) **pay sb. a visit** jm. einen Besuch abstatten
(to) **persuade** [pəˈsweɪd] überreden
(to) **place** stellen, legen, setzen
place: in the first place *hier:* sowieso
(to) **point (to)** zeigen (auf)
pottery [ˈpɒtərɪ] Töpferei
(to) **be prepared to do sth.** bereit sein, etwas zu tun
proof [pruːf] Beweis
prosecutor [ˈprɒsɪkjuːtə] (An-)Kläger/in
(to) **prove** [pruːv] beweisen, nachweisen
(to) **pull to pieces** in Stücke reißen
(to) **punch** [pʌntʃ] boxen

(to) **put** *hier:* ausdrücken
puzzled [ˈpʌzld] verwirrt, verdutzt

Q **quality** [ˈkwɒlətɪ] Eigenschaft; Fähigkeit

R **receipt** [rɪˈsiːt] Quittung, Beleg
(to) **reduce** [rɪˈdjuːs] reduzieren, verringern
regulation [regjʊˈleɪʃn] Verordnung, Vorschrift
relation [rɪˈleɪʃn] Beziehung, Verhältnis
relieved: (to) **be relieved** [rɪˈliːvd] erleichtert sein
(to) **remain** [rɪˈmeɪn] bleiben
rent [rent] Miete
responsible [rɪˈspɒnsəbl] verantwortlich
(to) **rest** [rest] ruhen
(to) **rise** [raɪz] erheben
room-mate (Zimmer-)Mitbewohner/in
rose → (to) **rise**
(to) **run a business/school** Geschäft/Schule leiten
(to) **run about** herumrennen
(to) **run one's fingers/hand through one's hair** sich mit den Fingern durch das Haar fahren
(to) **run rings round sb.** jn. in die Tasche stecken, mit jm. fertig werden

S **same as me** genauso wie ich
satisfy: (to) **be satisfied with sth.** [ˈsætɪsfaɪ] mit etwas zufrieden sein
scratch [skrætʃ] Kratzer, Schramme
(to) **serve** [sɜːv] servieren
shadow [ˈʃædəʊ] Schatten
sharp [ʃɑːp] schneidend
(to) **shoot back** zurückschnellen

(to) **shoot open** aufreißen
(to) **shrink: he felt himself shrink** [ʃrɪŋk] er hatte das Gefühl, daß er immer kleiner wurde
(to) **shrug** [ʃrʌg] die Achseln zucken
(to) **shut up** den Mund halten
silence [ˈsaɪləns] Ruhe, Schweigen
silent [ˈsaɪlənt] still, ruhig
silver [ˈsɪlvə] silbern
(to) **sleep on** weiter schlafen
(to) **sneeze** [sniːz] niesen
soft [sɒft] leise; sanft
soft drink alkoholfreies Getränk
solid [ˈsɒlɪd] stabil, kräftig
staff [stɑːf] Lehrerkollegium, Belegschaft
stage [steɪdʒ] Bühne
(to) **stand back** zurücktreten
(to) **stand up to sb.** jm. (mutig) gegenübertreten
stank → (to) **stink**
state Zustand
step [step] Stufe
(to) **step into/out** be-, heraustreten
stiff [stɪf] steif, starr
(to) **stink of sth.** stinken, übel riechen nach etwas
strong point starke Seite, Stärke
(to) **struggle** [ˈstrʌgl] sich winden, zappeln
subject Gesprächsgegenstand, Thema
sudden [ˈsʌdn] plötzlich
sum [sʌm] Summe
support [səˈpɔːt] Unterstützung
supposed: (to) **be supposed to do/be** [səˈpəʊzd] sollen
surely [ʃɔːlɪ] sicherlich
(to) **sweat** [swet] schwitzen
swing: to be in full swing [swɪŋ] voll im Gange sein

T (to) **take: What's taking you so long?** Warum dauert es so lange?

(to) **take a seat** Platz nehmen

(water) tap [tæp] (Wasser-)Hahn

(to) **tap** [tæp] (leicht) klopfen, pochen

tape [teɪp] (Ton-)Band

(to) **tax sth.** [tæks] für etwas Steuern zahlen

..., **that is** ..., heißt das

thoughtfully ['θɔːtfʊlɪ] gedankenvoll, nachdenklich

threatening ['θretnɪŋ] bedrohlich

(to) **thump** [θʌmp] hämmern, pochen

(to) **thunder** ['θʌndə] donnern

(to) **be trapped** [træpt] eingeschlossen, gefangen, verfangen sein

tray [treɪ] Tablett

treatment: He got the treatment. ['triːtmənt] Er hat seine Abreibung bekommen.

(to) **tremble** ['trembl] zittern

trial ['traɪəl] Prozeß, Verhandlung

trustee [trʌs'tiː] (Vermögens-)Verwalter/in, Treuhänder/in

(to) **turn down** leiser stellen

(to) **turn on/off** auf-, zudrehen

(to) **turn over** umdrehen, -wenden

U **underneath** [ʌndə'niːθ] unterhalb

unfortunate [ʌn'fɔːtʃnət] unglücklich; bedauerlich

unpleasant [ʌn'pleznt] unangenehm, unerfreulich

upper ['ʌpə] obere(r, s)

urgent ['ɜːdʒənt] drängend; hartnäckig

V **very last** allerletzte(r, s)
victim [ˈvɪktɪm] Opfer
visible [ˈvɪzəbl] sichtbar, erkennbar

W (to) **wander** [ˈwɒndə] ziehen, gleiten
(to) **wave** [weɪv] winken
way: that's the way it goes so kann es gehen
way: there's no way auf gar keinen Fall
week: a week on Wednesday Mittwoch in einer Woche
welcome: you're welcome (to do sth.) Sie dürfen gerne (…)
What for? Wozu?
What's that/he got to do with it? Was hat das/er damit zu tun?
while [waɪl] Weile
whistle [ˈwɪsl] Pfeife; Pfeifen
wide [waɪd] breit
(to) **widen** [ˈwaɪdn] (sich) erweitern
wooden [ˈwʊdn] Holz-, hölzern
word has got out es macht die Runde; es hat sich herumgesprochen
workshop [ˈwɜːkʃɒp] Werkstatt
(to) **wreck** [rek] zertrümmern

Y **yet** dennoch